D0206268

MEXICO:
SOME TRAVELS AND SOME TRAVELERS THERE

∴ Ruins ········ International Borders
• Towns ▲ Mountain Peaks
● Cities

UNITED
STATES

Río Grande

NTAL

O

Gulf of Mexico

Miguel
llende

Golfo
de Campeche

Mérida

CHICHÉN-
ITZÁ

erétaro

ico City
● Mt. Ixtacchihuatl
▲ ● Puebla ● Veracruz
Mt. Popocatepetl

Campeche ●

UXMAL

YUCATÁN

navaca Teotitlán

Oaxaca
MONTE
ALBÁN MITLA

Tuxtla
Gutiérrez

Villahermosa

PALENQUE

BELIZE

ulco

San Cristóbal
de las Casas

GUATEMALA HONDURAS

©1991 Claudia Carlson

A DESTINATIONS BOOK

MEXICO
Some Travels and
Some Travelers There

ALICE ADAMS

INTRODUCTION BY JAN MORRIS

A TOUCHSTONE BOOK
Published by Simon & Schuster
New York   London   Toronto   Sydney   Tokyo   Singapore

TOUCHSTONE
Simon & Schuster Building
Rockefeller Center
1230 Avenue of the Americas
New York, New York 10020

Copyright © 1990 by Alice Adams
Introduction Copyright © 1990 by Jan Morris

All rights reserved
including the right of reproduction
in whole or in part in any form.
First Touchstone Edition 1992
TOUCHSTONE and colophon
are registered trademarks of
Simon & Schuster Inc.
Design by Robert Bull Design
Manufactured in the United States of America

1   3   5   7   9   10   8   6   4   2

Library of Congress Cataloging-in-Publication Data
Adams, Alice, 1926–
Mexico : some travels and some travelers there / by
Alice Adams.
p.   cm.
1. Mexico—Description and travel—1981
I. Title.
F1216.5.A33   1991   91-21536
917.204'835—dc20   CIP

ISBN 0-671-76803-4
ISBN 0-671-79277-6 (pbk)

For Alison and Beverly and Bill.
Dan and Frannie and Howard and Mary-Ross.
Patricia, Pauline, Peter, and Phil.
Richard, and Robert.

Favorite companions.

CONTENTS

INTRODUCTION

by Jan Morris

MEXICO HAS a way, as Alice Adams says in this book, of traducing its chroniclers, so that each seems to be describing a different country. It is a matter of self-image, perhaps. Some writers see it as essentially a magic place, some as a scene of squalor or pathos, some as a merciful release from the constraints and conventions of more advanced (or ordinary) countries. Elsewhere, Mexico is an object lesson, or an awful warning, or a voice from the past, or a call to the future. It is the country within.

For Americans in particular, who are its immediate and intimate neighbors, Mexico seems to provide a kind of psychological sounding board against which they can measure their own sensibilities, and one might have guessed that Alice Adams, one of the most subtle and perceptive of contemporary novelists, would approach the country with particular capacity, exploring it for personal echoes, if not universal meanings. It is the great pleasure and surprise of this book that Ms. Adams shows us Mexico exactly as she finds it—no undercurrents, no hidden allusions, just a scrupulously fair account of her own responses, day by day.

Or rather, year by year, for she has been visiting the country for a very long time, and this book is really a kind of retrospective journal. It feels entirely unpremeditated.

Reading it is really like traveling with Alice Adams, sharing not only the sights and sounds and the travel experiences agreeable and unpleasant but the very conversations over dinner, the memories, the spontaneous ideas, even the mercifully vicarious pangs of indigestion. Moreover, since Ms. Adams travels sometimes with one friend, sometimes with another, we see out of the corners of our eyes, so to speak, the reactions of other travelers too.

It reminds me of the diaries of Virginia Woolf, in that the whole adds up to so much more than sum of the parts. The genre of literary travel writing (if genre it be) is infinitely varied in its techniques but straightforward in its purpose, which is to represent, in one way or another, the interaction between a place and a person. You may at first think, as you read the infinitely entertaining parts of this book, that you are learning a great deal about the person, not so much about the place: But you will find that, just as Virginia Woolf's gossipy and introspective journals add up to an evocation of an era, so the whole of Alice Adams's book turns out to be the portrait of a country after all.

So the subtle novelist surprises us twice, the apparently ingenuous jottings turn out to be more calculated than they seem, and Mexico—magical, sinister, pathetic, suggestive, the sounding board, the allegory—finds itself interpreted for once with absolute honesty.

PREFACE

OR A great many years, most of them spent in California, which is generally perceived as being close to Mexico, I had not the slightest wish to go there, to go south of the border. One reason for this was that I had spent a year of my early twenties in Europe, mostly in Paris—to which I yearned to return, but I was always much too broke to think of such trips. Mostly, though, I did not want to go to Mexico because of the people I knew who had been there and what they brought back with them: bright clay pots and gaudy scarves, jaunty statuary and carvings, costumed dolls and sombreros and smelly leather, and silver, pounds and pounds of silver jewelry. "Mexican" for me became synonymous with a certain artsy-craftsy kitsch—and it was a long time before I realized that those same people could undoubtedly go to Italy or Ireland and there too ferret out indigenous tastelessness. But by the time I knew that, I had made a few trips to Mexico myself and had begun to think about its multiple pleasures, its vast rewards. I did continue to notice and to find interesting, though, a strong tendency in travelers-to-Mexico to return with very much their own versions of Mexico—more so, I mean, than travelers to Europe or to Asia seem to do. It is as though there were something inherently passive in Mexico, inviting such imposition, and so I became almost as interested in these gringo versions of the country as in Mexico itself.

MEXICO HAS always been invasion-prone. I do not cite this as a fault but rather as a historical fact, her fate. Since the country was invaded by early Indian tribes and subsequently by almost every European country, most notably, of course, by Spain, and then countless times by us, the States (more than 100 invasions in all), it is extraordinary that anything approaching a national character should remain, in any recognizable form.

The most recent invaders have been the tourists, and it seems to me that these tourists have the same invasive instincts, not only in terms of plunder but also in a curious urge to make Mexico their own, to impose, that is, their own sensibilities on "Mexico" and to export it as their own product. Of course, this, to a certain degree, is true of travelers anywhere; still, the concepts of "England" or "Portugal" are somehow more daunting, more resistant to personal imposition, than those of "Mexico." Thus, Graham Greene's Mexico is almost pure Greene-land, and Malcolm Lowry's is mad, surreal, and dangerous. Less talented and far less imaginative writers have made of it a cheery, cozy, somewhat infantile, villagey place. A shrink I know thinks Mexico is sexy: "South of the border" to him means "below the belt." A character in one of Margaret Atwood's novels claims not to want to go to Mexico because it is too visceral, like a person turned inside-out, with all the veins and blood exposed.

A search for one's self, then, could be seen as among the (sometimes unconscious) reasons for going to Mexico—a self that one can bring home and trot out for marveling inspection.

This would to a degree be true anywhere, on any trip, of course; it is simply more marked, more nakedly apparent in travelers to Mexico. In extreme cases the country becomes a mirror in which only the self is viewed, as others succeed in finding only scraps of themselves, remnants of their fantasies.

Or, there are the travelers whose stance is one of total opposition to the country and its culture. My two favorites in this stubbornly resistant category were, first, a Texas lady whom I observed from my own safe balcony in Puerta Vallarta. This lady, of what used to be called a certain age, wore impeccably white clothes, a lot of heavy and probably real gold jewelry, and a mass of unreal golden curls. This was on a hot and sunny morning during a power failure; nothing was working, anywhere. No water, no nothing. Which the Texas lady could not entirely believe, and she went into a wonderfully infantile tantrum, stamping both white sandals and shouting to her captive audience of Mexican maids and workmen, "I don't care what you do! just fix it! *Fix It!!!*"

The second resister was a New York businessman whom I met by chance on the beach at Zihuatanejo. A considerably more controlled type than the Texas lady, he listened quietly as I extolled the virtues of a favorite beach restaurant and its seafood—although I could see a certain dangerous bulge to his eyes and a twitchy tightening of his mouth. My restaurant, Elvira's, was run by a woman named Ernestina, whose cooking, character, and general moral strength I also praised. At last this man could hear no more, and he burst out passionately, "Listen, that woman is doing for the restaurant business what the Boston strangler did for door-to-door sales."

I can only suppose that after eating at Elvira's he got terribly sick and blamed it on the cooking of Ernestina or the freshness of her fish; still, the judgment did seem harsh.

Which brings up an issue about which I think I should

digress: food, and illness. And I can only say that I have been extremely lucky; more than twenty trips and only one illness, and that came from Veracruz, a city with viruses so virulent that even Mexicans get sick there, I was told. I am reasonably cautious in Mexico; I don't eat street food, no matter how wonderful it smells, nor how appealingly proffered. But I do, in restaurants, eat fruit and salads. I am fairly careful about drinking water; mostly I drink iced tea, and beer and margaritas.

However, this must be an individual problem: I know a man who claims to get sick at the sight of a map of Mexico. It is my own idea that a somewhat casual attitude toward the whole issue is salutary, but I doubt if I could get much medical support for that view.

WE WHO love Mexico and love going there have our own quirks and odd inaccuracies, too. I first went to Mexico in the fifties, with my then-husband and very young son, Peter, who had just learned to swim at the local Y. A swimming trip for Peter was one of our somewhat curious excuses for a trip we could not afford; I think, actually, we longed for a version of Europe that was cheaper and more comprehensible. On that trip we drove down to Guaymas, where Peter and I spent marvelous hours in the embracing, clear green water—and where life was indeed very cheap. We found a cheap beach motel and subsisted mostly on shrimp and beer—and were told by older, more experienced Mexicophiles that we really had not been to Mexico at all.

My second trip was as caretaker to a friend who was to have an abortion in Tijuana. We flew to San Diego, where we met the connection, a nervous, pale-blond, brown-suited young man, in a hotel lobby. And he drove us (first protesting my presence—"I know how you girls like to talk"—until I assured him that we were so horrified by this procedure that we would never mention it) to Tijuana, then as now a giant, seedy-gaudy slum, full of bars and clubs and tourist shops, thousands of shops, full of trash—and then out to a very poor (even poorer than what we had seen already) neighborhood, to a dirty white stucco building labeled *Clinica Femina*. I was very scared and would have called it all off, but my friend was more afraid of telling her married lover (ironically, a "prominent" San Francisco surgeon) that she was still pregnant than she was of dubious medical practices. (The sheer panic involved in these occasions is something that men never know about, really.)

She later told me, however, that the doctor (the Mexican doctor) was exceptionally kind and gentle and apparently did a very good clean job—no later trouble. (But she has never gone back to Mexico, nor will she ever. She never saw the married surgeon after the Tijuana trip and has married happily—but has no children.)

AFTER THAT trip I, too, for quite another set of reasons, did not go back to Mexico—and then in the late sixties I began to go back again—and again and again. The reasons varied from a wish for a warm and reasonably cheap winter vacation, to curiosity about a country that I had barely begun to know, to an intense interest in artist Frida Kahlo. And, as a sort of sideline, I continued to find of absorbing interest the reactions to Mexico in North Americans traveling there—especially, of course, the reactions of those closest at hand: my own chosen traveling companions.

About traveling companions: Mine were all chosen with extreme care; they were all people whom I like/respect/find interesting and pleasant. And thus, in the pages that follow, I have very little of a negative nature to say about any of them.

But some combinations do seem more felicitous than others, and having tried most of them, I feel free to judge of this. Some familiar permutations are as follows:

1. Two couples. This can be risky, for all the obvious reasons. When I was a part of a couple we generally avoided such travel, only venturing it with ideal companions, whom I have called Rosemary and Paul.

2. A couple alone, married or romantically involved. This depends entirely, of course, on how well you are getting along—although I do think that travel puts a strain on even a good connection. For one thing you are too much together and probably unused to three meals a day together, not to mention all those decisions about when and where to have those meals. A close and wise friend of mine believes that travel is the ultimate sexual turnoff.

3. A single person with a couple. This poses certain risks; first off, the couple can make you feel lonely, if that is your tendency. Also, you have to be alertly tactful, not taking sides if they argue.

The other side of this combination—if you are a couple and invite a single person to come along—again calls for the exercise of tact, and at worst you have to assume a care-taker role. Obviously, you should look for a very healthy and very independent person (as part of a couple I once went to Italy with such a woman, a painter—a most successful trip).

I am not at all sure which works out best, but I can only say that I was most fortunate in my choices for the trips that I mention here—I would very happily go almost anywhere, again, with any of these people (whose names I have changed, for the most part, in the pages that follow).

I T IS almost a year now since I have been to Mexico, and I begin to feel a longing, a true need to go there again.

I think of certain colors, and certain smells, and the bare look of those withered mountains, as I am flying down from San Francisco.

And I begin to plan my next trip, to continue my love-hate relationship which, since I continue to go there, seems mostly love.

CHAPTER
ONE

ZIHUATANEJO A

FIRST WENT to Zihuatanejo one January, now fifteen years ago, having chosen that place for a somewhat odd group of negative reasons. The first was that I had a novel coming out that month, with new publishers, and a new editor, whom I had not met but who seemed brilliant but extremely young. This was my second novel; the first, nine years back, had not done well except in England, and I was running a little scared. I dreaded the reviews, or worse, their lack. Going away to a place that was both beautiful and remote would be a good solution I thought; insofar as a writer can ever ignore publication time, I believed that I almost could in Mexico. Also, January in San Francisco can be cold and raw and densely, darkly fogged (as it is now, even as I write, this January).

I had heard of Zihuatanejo, and I began to ask around.

At a party, some people whom I do not like at all said, "Oh, it's a terrible place, no one there, nothing to do." The F.'s, as I will call them, are socially hyperactive. It is crucial for them to be seen, to be mentioned in columns. They are what used to be called jet-setters and are quite as restlessly vacuous as that phrase suggests. And so, reasoning negatively (and quite correctly, as things turned out), I thought, Well, good, if the F.'s don't like it, I will probably love it there.

I eliminated Baja out of some notion (later to be proved wrong) that only huntin' fishin' shootin' types from Texas went there. Baja did not strike me as sufficiently "Mexican," whatever that was (and is: I am still trying to find out), to be appealing.

Puerto Vallarta was another obvious choice, easy to get to from the West Coast, popular with a variety of friends. Twice in successive years, however, I had been there with R. (the friend with whom I was to travel to Z.), and we had liked it less each successive year. On the idyllically secluded small beach of pure white sand where, our first year, we had shed our suits for a wonderful private swim, there was now a mountainous high-rise. We thought that if changes were taking place that rapidly, on a third trip we would not like it at all. Also, on our last afternoon in Vallarta, that second time, I almost drowned: There was an ugly, erratic tide, waves coming on so hard and fast that I kept being thrown down to the ocean floor, and then thrown down again. R. saved my life. An experienced beach person, he was able to gauge the waves precisely. He called out strong instructions—"Come in now"—and I managed to do what he said. Still, I was not left with a feeling that Vallarta was great for swimming.

The single possibly positive factor in the choice of Zihuatanejo was that some quite elderly people, the Martins, remote business acquaintances of R., said that they loved it there. They went every year for a month, R. told me. But even that was a negative, I thought; I considered the Martins too old and too "elegant" to count (once more, entirely wrong).

And so, from that cluster of advice and prejudice and hope, we chose Zihuatanejo and began to make plans.

The best way to get to Zihuatanejo at that time was by way of a bus from Acapulco, a city that I had seen enough of to know that I found it hateful. Wishing to avoid the repulsively fancy high-rise hotels, I booked us into a motel near the bus station, and recommended by one of my travel guides, which turned out to be quite terrible: We were greeted by scurrying cockroaches in the bathroom. But we got through the night somehow, and the next morning we arrived sleepless but in plenty of time for the first-class bus, the *Estrella de Oro*, for Zihuatanejo.

That first time the bus trip was extremely slow and very comfortable, fairly interesting and occasionally beautiful.

The bus itself was large and heavy, newish, air-conditioned; undoubtedly capable of considerable speed, it was driven with great caution by its proud driver. Also, despite this being a first-class bus, once out of Acapulco we stopped at almost all the off-highway tiny crossroads towns, with their bright shabby stucco houses (turquoise seems to be a favorite color for houses, very bright turquoise, in Mexico), their large church, little grocery store, small bar—their yellow rutted streets with clumps of small, staring, Mexican children, with huge, shining, solemn eyes. And scrawny dogs who thump their tails in the dust, and a scratching red chicken or two.

From time to time a group of soldiers stationed at the roadside would stop the bus and board—very young men, with enormous guns and belts of bullets. They were looking for arms or drugs, I guess, though it is hard to see how they could have spotted either, walking through the bus and poking at an occasional piece of luggage.

A couple of hours out of Acapulco the route veers toward the coast, and we then entered an endless series of coconut palm forests, great gray trunks through which we could catch an occasional bright-blue glimpse of the sea, the shining Pacific. Down among those palms are the extremely small thatch-roofed shacks of the tenant farmers; above are the thick, pale-green, spiny fronds, rattling like snakes in the warm sea breezes.

This uninterrupted, unvarying landscape lasts for several hours, which is fairly boring if you've seen it before—until you come to the actual coast, to beaches. Long, white, unpopulated strips of sand and small blue waves. Tantalized by that first sight, we could not wait to get there.

Our first view of the actual town of Zihuatanejo was quite unpromising, though: a small dirty crossroads, a couple of shabby stores, a skinny dog scratching in some mud. Fleetingly, I wondered if the awful F.'s could be right, that Zihuatanejo really was a terrible place that no sane person would like. We wandered about in a somewhat bewildered way, telling ourselves that areas surrounding bus stations are always terrible (God knows this is true enough). At last, along with some other Americans from the bus who were similarly confused, we found a cab, which we all agreed to share for the ride to our various hotels.

Fairly quickly, then, we drove up and out of town and onto a weedy, rocky cliff above the water, the brilliant, glimmering sea. Bougainvillea, all colors, flowed down that cliff, to the sand. We could see the beach and already, from that distance, I knew that I had begun to fall in love.

The other couple's hotel came first, and then a little distance further on our cab started down an odd spiral driveway, fairly steep, down to what seemed to be a huge balcony overlooking the sea. (That balcony always made me think of Dick Diver, in *Tender Is the Night,* saying goodbye to the beach at the Côte d'Azur, with his curious gesture of blessing.) There was a registration desk and people in charge: two Germans, a man and a woman—he vague and somewhat deranged in aspect, with a wandering expression; she plump and kind and efficient. There were several Mexicans, some pretty girls behind the desk and a few boys standing about in their loose khaki clothes, seeming to await instructions.

Having registered, we were then led by one of the boys

(they were terribly young, and strong, very agile with heavy bags) down past another, smaller balcony, cantilevered out from the hill, with tables and chairs and a very long, clearly well stocked bar. We went past rows of attached small cabins, all with balconies. Down and down to the room that was ours, with its small porch-balcony. Room 13. Quite plain and bare, with its wide windows looking past the porch, and down and out to the sea.

And, as we almost instantly discovered (we heard their voices), immediately next door, in Room 14, were the Martins, the elderly couple of Zihuatanejo regulars, about whom I had by then forgotten. Right next door. What is surprising is that even then, so close to people we more or less knew and who were roughly twenty-five years older than ourselves, we did not take alarm at such proximity. (R. in his way is a friendlier person than I am; he would have been less likely to object, and besides, he already knew them.)

I was actually thinking less of the Martins than of the fact that just then, on first sight, I knew this was the most beautiful place I had ever been, or seen. I loved it.

The town of Zihuatanejo is actually on a large horseshoe-shaped bay, bounded at the horizon by large rocky promontories, from which feathery trees lean up and out into the sky. Small fishing boats move slowly across the water, out there in the shining distance, and occasionally (but never on that first visit, as I remember it) a huge cruise ship would anchor there, an awful intrusion, with its most unwelcome load of the wrong, worst kind of tourist.

Our hotel, some two or three miles out of town, up on its bluff, overlooked that shining bay and a long white beach. Around a rocky curve we could look back to the town, low-lying, indistinct, marked mostly by its cluster of fishing boats. At the other end of the beach there rose abruptly a steep hill of jungle growth, green-gray shades of exotic, possibly dangerous, vegetation. More immediately, all around the tiers of rooms (ours was the lowest tier, closest to the beach and the sea), flowers bloomed and thrived, mostly bougainvillea, and trumpet vines, and various trees whose names I never learned.

I loved everything about it there, instantly, including the somewhat haphazard, slightly jerry-built nature of the dwelling structures. I found the rather basic, primitive equipment deeply appealing: What, really, do you need in a hotel room beyond a bed and table, a closet and functioning bathroom? I liked not having a phone or TV; we had instead a balcony porch with a table, a couple of chairs—and the loveliest view in the world, I thought. I could be perfectly happy there, I imagined; and for a number of years (in fact thirteen—make what you will of all these thirteens), for a couple of weeks each year, I was. Perfectly happy.

THIS WAS the pattern of our days in Zihuatanejo: We would wake and get up, I think around seven-thirty or eight, and go down to the beach for a swim, on some days swimming more vigorously than on others, out into the clear, flat, delicious water—looking back to the beach where, often, solitary runners sped or jogged along the packed wet sand, walkers kept up a brisk pace, and occasional groups of dogs ran about, nipping or trying to nip at the legs of retreating sandpipers, or simply at waves.

This was also the hour at which to claim a *palapa,* one of the small, round, thatch-roofed shelters with a couple of rickety white chairs, for the rest of the day. Emerging from the water, drying off a little, we would then leave one of our towels and maybe yesterday's newspaper on one of those chairs (the same chair every day; everyone had his favorite).

This was the custom, and for many years, with minor rebellious skirmishes with newcomers, it worked out well.

Back up in our room, after showers and dressing (in a very few light clothes: it was already very warm), we headed along the path that crossed that hill, past another tier of rooms, past flowers, glimpses of the water, and waiting beach—toward the dining room. Looking forward to breakfast, and to the day.

The dining room, like the entrance area, was essentially a roofed-over platform, overlooking the lower hillside, vines, and clumps of palm trees—looking out to sea. Breakfast there was semibuffet: From a central table you gathered up a plate full of bright fresh fruit—papayas and pineapple, melons and bananas. Maids came around to take orders for the second course—mostly pretty, dark young village girls whose names we gradually learned, only to have them be replaced by others the following year.

After the fruit came various forms of eggs, Mexican and/or North American, bacon, and sausages—you could have almost anything, including oatmeal or French toast or pancakes. I liked the rolls best, *bolillos,* fine-textured and slightly sweet, always very fresh.

That first year, and for several subsequent years, families of cats, of various ages and sizes, roamed the dining room. Cats to whom R. and I fed a great deal of bacon—out of sight of Carlos, the mean, rather druggy-looking German owner, who hated cats and loved only his police dogs.

Sometimes we observed the Martins as they entered the dining room, in their always impeccably clean and very white clothes, as they took their preferred, secluded table—but we did not speak to them, at breakfast. "We think it's wonderful that you're here, and we so look forward to seeing you for cocktails at seven-thirty," Celeste Martin said to us early on in our stay. And, taking it further (in case we had missed the point): "I never speak to anyone before breakfast." Which made it all extremely easy, and possible.

On some days we were able to get a newspaper in the dining room, a *Mexico City News,* from one of the small brown vendors, little boys who darted among the tables and struck hard bargains for pesos.

Then, back to our room, for a slow change into bathing suits, perhaps some reading on the deck, and then a descent to the beach, to our private and reserved *palapa.*

The next step was a walk to the end of the beach—in the course of which we passed several lunch-serving beach shacks and a few hotels that, down at beach level, we found much less appealing than our own. And a number of other strollers, in various stages of health or decrepitude—mostly American, although it is somewhat hard to decipher people's nationalities in bathing suits, unless you hear them speak. And always a host of skittering sandpipers, whose gait reminded us a lot of our oldest cat—she too skittered, in fact almost until the day she died, quite recently.

At the far end of the beach some kids with trailer trucks, and babies, and dogs were camped out, that spot being their Zihuatanejo, as that hotel where we always went is irrevocably mine. I imagined their sitting out on the beach at night to enjoy the sunsets and then the show of stars, as we did from our elevated balcony.

Back at our *palapa,* shedding shirts and hats, whatever, we hurried out into the water for a swim that was entirely unlike our early-morning dip. The water was warmer by now, and more people were out in the waves; even, sometimes, a speedboat pulling a water-skier flashed by, perilously close to the swimmers, I thought. But the water still had that magic quality of buoyancy, lapping, caressing our skins—it was at the same time both warm and cool—as it was also both green and blue.

Social life on the beach was fairly loose. Some couples, close friends from home, arrived together and shared a *palapa* every day. One year a large group from Chicago arrived, and they did everything together, and no one else liked them at all—they were extremely noisy, and one of them smoked a cigar, at all times. More usual encounters were friendly and rather brief, a pause at another *palapa,* some information or local gossip exchanged. More than anyone else on the beach, the Martins tended to keep to themselves, and perhaps to a certain extent, in that as well as in other, more subtle ways, they set an example to us; we, too, tended to stay more or less apart.

At various times in the course of the morning, various people would decide that it was time for a beer; it was so extremely hot, and it must be almost noon, mustn't it? And oh! the sharply gratifying, richly bitter thrust of that first taste. It was marvelous; no subsequent sips or thirsty gulps were ever quite so good.

We might swim again, might conceivably have another beer (R. more often than I); we might read again for a while in our *palapa*—and then it was time for lunch.

Our favorite place was a lean-to shack, up on a crude concrete floor, just at the bottom of the stairs up to our hotel. Elvira's. It was run by a very dark-skinned, gypsy-looking woman, Ernestina—and her lazy, dapper husband. Several children, some theirs and others more or less borrowed, also helped with the work of the restaurant. These people had squatters' rights to their shack, which was infuriating to Carlos. Gnarled, moth-eaten old parrots in rickety cages guarded the entrance; on the way out we would feed them soda crackers.

Fresh seafood. We had clams and oysters and shrimp and sometimes lobster. Fish soup, fish salads, fish sandwiches. But the best, the specialty of the house, of which we talked and sometimes dreamed in San Francisco, was the *huachinango al mojo de ajo,* red snapper cooked in a lot of garlic, in very dark-brown hot oil, and eaten with slices of onion and tomato and avocado, with fresh tortillas. Perched there in the path of sea breezes, swatting at flies, we would drink more beer and eat. And eat, and eat.

After all that food we hurried back into the ocean, something our mothers would not have approved at all. We alternated swimming and lounging beneath the *palapa* for an hour or so until siesta time, the long, restorative, mid-to-late-afternoon nap, beneath the large white tropical fan, a fan that always worked.

And, after that long nap, another swim. But in the small interval between our nap and going down to swim we would pause for a while to sit outside and watch the sunset from our porch, each night an absolutely fresh procession of colors above the cliff that bounded our horizon, the gate to our bay. As, down below us on the beach, the Martins began their evening walk—we could indeed have set our watches by them: she, small and determined, walking ahead; he, tall and slower, a few short paces behind her.

During that swim the water was perfectly flat and bright, a dark, wavering mirror. We swam out for a while and then turned back to scan the early-evening sky for stars. Usually we could see at least two or three, and we made something of a contest out of this—who could see the most stars first. R. almost always won.

Dressing for dinner was more of a project than one might imagine, given the somewhat run-down look of the place, but the Martins, especially Celeste, set a very high standard indeed. She wore wonderful long, pale, gauzy skirts or light silk trousers, and wonderful jewelry, a lot of it bought down there, silver beads and small white bones strung along a silver chain, and turquoise, lots of turquoise. We showered, then, and dressed as best we could—and appeared next door at precisely 7:30. By this time the sky was all dark, and there were millions of visible bright stars.

In the evenings, along with her filmy clothes, Celeste wore what were obviously wigs—soft and silver-white, all waved and puffed out, but nevertheless wigs. During the day she tied white silk scarves rather tightly around her head; with her strong, bold features she looked a lot like Isak Dinesen, I always thought. At some point (I am sure this was not over cocktails) she explained to me what I suppose I might have guessed, that she had lost most of her hair to chemotherapy. She had had cancer of the pancreas about five years earlier, a cancer from which almost no one recovers, but she did, Celeste won out. "I just decided not to die," she said, and I believed her. (Doctors often refuse to believe this story of Celeste, who lived for more than fifteen years after having had pancreatic cancer, at seventy. One doctor even assured me that she must have been wrong about her diagnosis, but she was not; Celeste was almost never wrong.)

After the one quite ceremonious drink on the Martins's porch, the four of us would proceed very slowly upward to the bar, where we took a table near the outer edge, the railing. Near the view. A few dim spotlights shone down on the gray-white sand, the ghostly beach, and lights flickered far out on the black, black water, here and there. Celeste drank a rum and water (less than half an ounce of rum; she left permanent instructions with the bartender, Mario), and the rest of us had margaritas—of course the best in the world, the sweetest, sourest, the most tart margaritas ever made. (I must at this point give my recipe for the very worst of all possible margaritas, which someone, a doctor, actually served us once: Take a bottled margarita and mix it well with cracked ice *and* a bottle of 7-Up. I know, hard to believe, but this actually happened.)

Dinner itself was perhaps the most unremarkable part of the day. Usually there was a choice between fish and some vaguely Germanic meat dish, some schnitzel or goulash, neither very successful. Thus, we tended to eat very lightly at night, the recommendation of nutritionists, I think. And just as well, after all that daytime food.

The night view from the dining room, though, was truly glamorous: lights glimmering down through palm fronds, down to the bone-gray beach, to the shining, black, flat water.

And then we went to bed. I remember being kept awake by heavy, pounding surf sometimes at the start of a visit, but after a night or so I was used to it. We generally slept well and got up the next morning eager to repeat the day before—got up more relaxed, happier, a little more tan.

THERE WERE occasional variations. For instance, always on the first day of our stay we would walk down into the town for some shopping.

The road arched up high above the sea; we looked down a rocky, weedy, flower-strewn cliff to the brilliant blue. On our way we passed a couple of hotels that were newer, smaller, and much more garish than ours, walked down to a very small stream, almost dried up. A concrete bridge, and then the town: straggling, one-story (a very few two-story) houses and stores, bars and restaurants, all jumbled together, along muddy, cobbled, or just plain dirt streets.

Unless a cruise ship happened to be anchored at Zihuatanejo, there were not many tourists, I guess just barely enough to keep the local industry going. The stores sold the ordinary and requisite silver jewelry and long lacy cotton dresses, straw hats and bandannas, film and suntan lotions. We walked about, always commenting on the fact that there were no good postcards to be had—this seemed amazing, in such a beautiful, eminently photogenic place. And we bought our supplies: some vodka and tonic, things to munch at drink time, and sometimes for me a long dress, or a hat for R., some bandannas.

Then we took a taxi back to our hotel and hurried down to the beach, from which we never wished to be away, for long.

A NOTHER, CONSIDERABLY more strenuous, variation on our routine was a hike around the curve of the bay to a beach known as Los Gatos; I have never found out why—I cannot imagine cats there. This excursion involved a walk to the end of the beach, a mile or so. Then a pause for putting on some sort of shoes, and then a fairly prolonged clambering over some very steep, very sharp rocks. Sometimes among these rocks we would meet a couple of Mexican boys, small and lithe and barefoot, scurrying like monkeys as we labored on. A couple of times we met an ancient Indian woman, with dark withered brown skin and infinitely old, dark-brown eyes, in one of the elaborately layered costumes that the local Indians wore, including all the vendors on the beach: layers of white flounces above more layers of dark-blue skirts. And barefoot: On gnarled dark-brown leather feet she moved across sharp rocks, with a shy smile at the pale, clumsy strangers, in their heavy rubber-and-canvas shoes.

Los Gatos is a small, rather homey beach, where mostly

Mexican vacationers sit under a long, communal *palapa* and drink beer and eat mountainous plates of raw oysters (we used to do that too, until we began to think seriously of hepatitis and lost our nerve). Out in the shallow water small children paddle and play, as their fat grandmothers in black wool bathing suits that do not quite fit sit among the tiny waves, and splash themselves, like grandmothers at Jones Beach or La Jolla. Several small boats were usually anchored there at a little wooden dock, tied with pieces of rope, waiting for business.

Walking on past Los Gatos, as we sometimes did, toward the rocky point that formed one of the boundaries of our bay, we came to a curious semipopulated area. For years, a resort had been in the process of being built there: thatch-roofed sleeping quarters built high up on stilt supports, very tropical in their aspect. It had seemed to have a succession of owners, this place, beachcomber-looking Americans, mostly, men with lonely wives—for all I know, by now it is finished and thriving. Some years there was an operative bar out there at the end, where we would stop for a beer. Other years, the bar was there but no person, nor any beer.

Sometimes, after lunch at Los Gatos, we would walk back to our own beach, back over all those difficult sharp rocks; other years we hired one of the little boats (for two or three dollars, I think) whose owner, revving up the small motor, would take us not very fast across all that water to within several yards of our own beach, at which point we would have to jump out and wade in to shore.

A NOTHER EXCURSION was a cab ride over to Ixtapa, the much younger and somewhat sleazy sister city of Zihuatanejo. Ixtapa is all very new—new flashy high-rise condominiums, swimming pools with island bars in the middle, where you swim up for a fancy drink. Across the way is an extensive rolling green golf course. Everything in Ixtapa looks more expensive than anything in Zihuatanejo, and it attracts a very different group: younger, swingier, noisier people, richer people, in brighter, trendier clothes. We used to drive over there and walk around rather snobbishly, sometimes staying for lunch in one of the hotel restaurants, other years contenting ourselves with a single margarita, as we remarked on how crowded their beach was (it really was, body to body), how noisy the people. Et cetera.

However, the advent of the Hotel Camino Real to some degree changed all that. It is an extremely handsome, impressive structure, worth seeing. Like the Camino Real in Mexico City, it was designed by a pupil of Luís Barragán, the famous and talented Mexican architect. Huge sweeps of plain plaster wall, painted a bright orange-umber, with here and there an accent of deep bright blue. The scale is very grand, Aztec-looking; one could easily feel lost there, if not dwarfed (possibly not, though, in one's room). There are several swimming pools and an elevator down to the hotel's own private beach, which is quite uncrowded, white and beautiful, looking out to small, sharp, rock islands. Also, there is an excellent and attractive restaurant, all blue-tiled—and breezily open to that same view.

And so the yearly jaunt to Ixtapa became less condescending; it indeed became quite a treat. (I even think, especially at this writing, of going to stay there and of visiting Zihuatanejo—not exactly furtively, but somewhat on the sly.)

T HAT FIRST year in Zihuatanejo, after a couple of days the Martins announced that they wanted to take us out to dinner: The next night was their wedding anniversary, their forty-fifth. (They had eloped to Reno in 1930; I never learned the reasons, if there were reasons, for the elopement, which seemed out of character for them both.) Some people had opened a hotel around the bay, more or less on the way to Los Gatos, which they had heard served good dinners. We were to bring sneakers for the rocky part, Celeste instructed.

The restaurant turned out to be just at the start of the rocks, up some slab stone steps to a stone-arched room, all open to the night breezes and to the sea, to those incredibly romantic night views. We had French champagne (an extreme, most expensive luxury in Mexico) and Caesar salad and local lobster (unfortunately very tough), and we all exclaimed that everything was the best we had ever had. (Celeste was like that; she insisted that the late years of her life were far better than the early ones, and I suppose that this could have been true—I later learned a little of early trouble with Charles. And R., who had known her for years, told me that Celeste with her wigs was much more beautiful now than she had been as a younger woman. Still, I know that she had this strong habit of positive thought—worth emulating, I sometimes remind myself.)

The bartender-maître d' that night (also the owner, as things turned out) was a dashing, mustachioed, somewhat thickset, and graceful man named Arnaldo. He seemed distressed to hear that we had walked from our hotel—the Martins looked even older and more frail than in fact they were, especially at night. And so Arnaldo insisted on driving us home in his jeep.

He took a road home through the jungle that I never saw before or after that, but at the time it was exciting and a little scary; we were driving on what was hardly wider than a path, with thick vines and trees all around us and above, the spangled sky just visible, barely. It seemed to me that Arnaldo was a little drunk (a supposition that his later sad history seemed to confirm); we raced through the jungle until the road stopped abruptly at our beach, near Ernestina's restaurant, and the steps up to our rooms, Rooms 13 and 14.

Saying goodnight to the Martins, we began in a somewhat manic and sentimental way to talk about their fiftieth anniversary, five years hence. What a marvelous event to look forward to, I thought.

THAT TRIP was indeed the first of what became annual jaunts; each January, calculatedly in time for the Martins's anniversary, we would head down to Mexico—to which I looked forward all year, sometimes counting the days, like a child before Christmas. The process of getting there was considerably improved by the advent of a Zihuatanejo-Ixtapa airstrip, which obviated the need for what had become a most boring bus ride from Acapulco.

Aside from that innovation, for several years nothing much changed. Some of the same people showed up each year, some of whom we knew and talked to, had an occasional drink or dinner with. Others we simply saw and recognized, and gossiped about, speculatively, among ourselves. ("Was he with that same guy last year? He looks different. No, that can't be his daughter, don't be silly.")

Sometimes, at home in San Francisco, we saw the Martins; we were friends, but I always felt that our essential relationship took place in Mexico. In my image of Celeste, she is seated on her terrace, her head wrapped in one of her fresh white linen scarves, and she is leaning forward to stare intently at a small yellow butterfly that is perched on the large red flower of a trumpet vine.

Or, she and Charles are walking down on the beach, at sunset, she so small and determined and erect, and he following, thin and leaning forward in her direction.

As I set my watch.

CHAPTER
TWO

ZIHUATANEJO B

HAPPY AS we were in Zihuatanejo, a fit of restiveness would occasionally set in. Mexico is such an enormous country, we would say to each other; surely we should at least try another place. In fact, that same mood seemed to strike many of the Zihuatanejo regulars from time to time; often, after a year's absence, those people would show up again, always saying, "Well, such a disappointment, we couldn't wait to get back here." Or some such pious sentiment.

Nevertheless, struck by that mood, one year, the year that was to be our fifth in Zihuatanejo, we went first to Puerto Escondido, far to the south, beyond Acapulco—in the province of Oaxaca. Which turned out to be a considerable mistake, all around.

We went there with friends from Santa Barbara, Rosemary and Paul, old, reliable, good pals; this part of our plan, at least, was not a mistake. And someone we knew in San Francisco had heard of a new hotel, into which we booked ourselves—for New Year's Eve. (You see? a crazy plan from the start.) This hotel was up on a bluff, a few miles out of town, and it was simultaneously new and coming apart at the seams. The room to which we were led had not been made up, nor, it turned out, had any of the other rooms. The hotel restaurant was not quite functioning. Unfortunately, this all took place on New Year's Eve: Out on the grounds there was a very noisy party—and the next day nothing had been cleaned up; empty Scotch and champagne bottles lay about all over, along with soggy, half-eaten sandwiches, too far gone for even the ravenous, scavenging birds, the skinny, famished dogs.

Down the cliff, though, there was a beautiful white beach—and the water was marvelous, green and clear and magically buoyant. Mexican water.

Our plan was to spend only a couple of days there in Escondido and then to proceed on to Zihuatanejo—most important, to get there in time for the Martins's fiftieth wedding anniversary. Having flown down from Oaxaca in a DC-3, our intention was to rent a car in Escondido and drive along the coast to Zihuatanejo. We were united in wishing not to retrace our steps by air; not, that is, to fly back to Oaxaca, to Mexico City, and then down to Zihuatanejo, though that would clearly have been the more sensible way to go.

It would have been especially sensible since, as things turned out, there were no rental cars in Escondido. No agency, no cars. It seemed that our only choice was a bus (second class) to Acapulco, where we could change and pick up the old faithful *Estrella de Oro* (first class) to Zihuatanejo. Rosemary and Paul are vastly good-natured people, both of them; they rarely complain, and so traveling with them tends to bring out one's own better nature. We all said, Well, fine, an adventure, the second-class bus to Acapulco. How interesting; it won't last long. Everyone had been very vague as to time, and I have no idea what we expected.

We were advised to appear at a certain crossroads at a specified time, in order to get good seats. We did just that and agreed among ourselves that the bus really did not look too bad. But the problem, almost immediately apparent, was overcrowding (what airlines call "overbooking"). We stopped at literally every crossroads that we passed, picking up people and depositing far fewer than we picked up. People packed the aisles, lurching back and forth as the bus lurched. Kind Rosemary held someone's wet baby for a while, and we all at least considered giving our seats to older, less vigorous people, but somehow did not. And we all felt conspicuous in the Levi-denim shirt casualness of our dress; the Mexicans were mostly all dressed up for travel, the men in white shirts and dark suits, the young women in high heels and tight skirts. Older women dressed sensibly in loose-fitting skirts, old shoes.

Also, the Mexican passengers had mostly brought food along; those who had not managed to reach through the windows to buy treats from the vendors who circled the bus at some of our numerous stops. We had not brought or thought of bringing any food, and though it looked and smelled better and better as time went on, we did not dare eat that vended food—we knew it was dangerous for gringos. We got hungrier and hungrier.

And: We all began to wonder about getting to Acapulco in time for the 5:30 bus, which was our intention. "Oh, maybe we can take a swim there," we had said earlier, imagining too much time on our hands in Acapulco. But this trip seemed literally to be taking forever.

We did, though, somehow get to Acapulco about five o'clock. There was then a problem that we had not counted on at all, that of getting across town to the first-class station. I suggested, half-facetiously, that we might do well to stay where we were, take another second-class bus to Z., what the hell? No one listened, though as things turned out that would have been a very good idea.

To our cab driver we stressed the need for haste—we had a bus to catch. He sped along dutifully, and on the Boulevard Miguel Alemán, beside the fabled blue Acapulco Bay, he was stopped by a cop and arrested for speeding. It was then discovered that none of his papers were in order: no more driving for our driver that day.

We piled out with our luggage, there in the middle of the busy boulevard, and tried to flag down another cab.

Which we finally did, and we arrived at the *Estrella de Oro* station at about 5:35.

Our bus had indeed already departed. However, such luck! There was another bus for Zihuatanejo, which would leave at 8:30. Which meant getting to Z. very late, but still it seemed okay (although, as I did not say, we still would have done better to stick with second class). We went out and found an awful Tahitian-looking restaurant, prettily situated in an outdoor grove of palms, where we greedily ate soggy shrimp, egg rolls, whatever, and drank some beer.

When we got back to the station about eight, thinking that we had plenty of time, an enormous, seething crowd had filled the departure room. They could not all be going to Z., we said among ourselves; if so, there might not be enough room. Well, all those people were at least going in our direction, if not actually to Z., and indeed, we did not get on that bus.

But: There was another bus at 10:30—which, although we stayed right where we were, we did not get on.

And another at 11:45—same story.

We all spent the night in a truly horrible small hotel: thin, damp, undoubtedly unclean sheets, and almost no water—and the next morning at 7:30, breakfastless, we boarded the bus for Zihuatanejo. Where, after many stops (first-class buses are second class as soon as they leave the station, is my conclusion), we arrived just before noon. In time for a swim, and a beer, and lunch.

And in time for the Martins's anniversary.

I had explained to Rosemary and Paul about our

strangely formal-intimate relationship with the Martins; I further explained that Celeste had some odd and quite unpredictable reactions to people—what I meant and did not quite say was that Celeste might very well take against Paul, who has a full beard and a very outspoken way of talking (he is, in fact, a distinguished judge, actually his speech is wonderfully literate, as well as frank). I also meant that the Martins might want to celebrate their anniversary with us alone. However, once more time, unpredictably, Celeste liked both Rosemary and Paul very much indeed, on sight, and she invited them to the celebration.

Which was most splendid. Charles had arranged for a fireworks show on the beach; we watched from the upper bar, and it was fabulous. Great flowers of fire, spurting up high into the black night sky, going on and on—until the marvelous finale: a big 50. In lights, in the sky.

For dinner we had French champagne and tough local lobster. The champagne was a present from Carlos (in all the years that I knew him, if slightly, he made no better gesture, in my view). I sneaked a lot of lobster to the cats, who were bold enough to approach, even with Carlos in the offing. Everyone had a wonderful time.

A FEW DAYS after that Rosemary and Paul departed, and a day or so after that Charles got sick—nothing serious, Celeste assured us, coming into the dining room to order trays and refusing any help from us. But he had to keep to his quarters, as it were, for the next week or so.

At around that time R. and I had become mildly friendly with a young German couple, Helene and Otto. She, about ten years younger than he, had studied in the States; both spoke perfect English, and Otto's Spanish was exceptional;

we heard him on the beach, talking to passing Mexican fishermen.

One night, in a fit of restlessness, maybe impatience with the hotel's bad dinners, R. and I went into town for dinner, a thing we almost never did. When we got back, fairly late, there, on the path from the reception desk down to the rooms, were Helene and Otto, as though waiting for us. They had a local newspaper in hand and were visibly upset, and they told us this story:

A young boy, Ernesto, seventeen, was being held in the local jail for the murder of a rich plantation owner. Ernesto was the son of a tenant farmer, extremely poor; a year earlier, at sixteen, he had witnessed the murder of his father by this rich owner, a reputed drunk. Neither killing was disputed; there had been witnesses in both cases. One of the owner's guards had managed to wound Ernesto.

What could we do to help Ernesto, maybe to save him?

W HAT WE did was go to the jail to see him, Helene and Otto and I. (R., for private reasons, chose not to go along).

The jail was a small white structure, behind the city hall. Down in the town, near the harbor and the city beach.

Otto talked us in, with elaborate blandishments and explanations of our interest in Ernesto. I was an American journalist, in Otto's version, and Helene a German filmmaker (which she now is). I think the big cop, with his heavy mustache and array of pistols, was afraid not to let us go in—God knows what we would have said or done, internationally.

A door was unlocked and then locked behind us. I was scared. We were in jail, a Mexican jail, a bare, dirt-floored room, in which men and women sat about and smoked and stared. Toilets for each were curtained off on opposite walls. One fierce-eyed legless man sat there on a tattered blanket, muttering softly.

Ernesto was brought out to us.

Ernesto: a very thin, pale boy. One arm wounded and in a sling. He had lost a lot of blood, and in that lightless room he looked green.

Otto spoke to him at some length, telling how we had read about him, saying that we thought he was very brave. Could we bring him anything?

Ernesto, with some hesitation, at last said that he would like some comic books.

The next day we came back, with comic books and candy and a shirt (apparently you can bring anything you want to prisoners in Mexican jails); this time we were allowed to talk to Ernesto in the big cop's office. We did not have to go into the jail room, but not much more was said. Ernesto came from Petatlán, he told us, a tiny town that I remembered from the bus trip; we had stopped there for several minutes, at a point when the smallest delay seemed unbearable. Ernesto told us that his mother would come to see him soon. He did not know when his trial would be.

A couple of days after that, a Sunday, there, indeed, was Ernesto's mother, a small, dark, fearful-looking woman: her husband murdered, her son an avenging killer. We pooled our pesos, Helene and Otto and I, which came to quite a lot, and Otto persuaded her to take them—for the bus trips to see Ernesto, he said—and indeed all that traveling must have been quite a costly procedure for her.

With the mother was a dark young man, quite handsome and nice, who introduced himself as a cousin of Ernesto's. He was wearing a police uniform and explained to us that he was a law student, putting himself through law school with police work. He further explained that there was now a contract out on Ernesto: The brothers of the dead plantation owner, them-selves all very rich and powerful, big drinkers, wanted him dead. Anyhow. Anywhere.

We saw no way to get Ernesto out of jail and into our own custody, as it were. All that we could do, we thought, was to create in the town a sense that he was backed, that anything that happened to Ernesto was being watched, internationally. Thus, before leaving Zihuatanejo that year, we spoke to every-one we knew there, urging them to stop by the jail for a minute with a comic book, or a candy bar, anything for Ernesto. And we asked that when they were about to leave, they would ask other people to help continue this process.

I have no idea how long all this went on, nor how effec-tive it was; I only know that no one from the evil planter's group got to Ernesto in jail, but I am not sure that we can take credit for that. Later in the year I got a letter from Helene and Otto, enclosing pictures of Ernesto at a sort of juvenile deten-tion center. Otto had written to the jail in Zihuatanejo (a jail that was eventually destroyed, in the earthquake of eighty-five). The juvenile authorities had written back to him, mostly expressing pride in their facilities but also mentioning their belief that Ernesto was doing well in the school that they provided. (Ironically, he might very possibly never have gone to school had he not spent time in jail.)

Later, as I have said, "Helene" became a successful and famous film director. I saw her again in San Francisco, and she told me that she and Otto had "broken up," that she was with someone else.

As, eventually, R. and I broke up, but that is another story and one that I am not inclined to tell.

CHAPTER
THREE

ZIHUATANEJO C

FOR QUITE a few years we continued to go to Zihuatanejo each January, always staying in Room 13, next door to the Martins, and always seeing them in that somewhat formal yet increasingly intimate way. And also seeing various other people who came and went, and having various adventures—though none quite so sensational as an involvement in a murder, and time spent in jail.

ONE YEAR, in the Mexico City airport, we fell into conversation with a young, just-married couple, she American, he English, who, like us, were waiting for the plane to Zihuatanejo (this could be a very long process, always reminding us of the second-class bus history). They were headed for Z., for the deep-sea fishing, which we had heard was great. We, of course, knew about this; other people were sometimes surprised that we did not even bother to fish. They were staying in our hotel, these two, who were very appealing. She was a strong, sixties-American woman, he rather thin and wispy, a physicist.

We ran into them a day or so later in the bar, where we were having a drink with Celeste, Charles being slightly sick again. This new couple spoke again of fishing, and Celeste told us what we had not known before: Charles used to love to fish, in his Minnesota boyhood.

And, a few days later, Charles by then being well, early one morning we all set out together in a small rented fishing boat, for a day of deep-sea fishing (neither R. nor I had ever fished significantly in our lives). In theory we would catch our lunch, which the two young Mexicans who ran the boat would cook for us, on the island toward which we were headed.

A beautiful clear day—as almost all the days in Zihuatanejo were beautiful, and clear. We crossed the bay, the low-lying town to our right, invisible Los Gatos Beach over to our left; and we passed through the gate, passed the sharp rocky cliff, with its lacy, feathered-out trees, behind which we watched the sun set every night, and headed out to sea. We had a good view of the Camino Real in Ixtapa, which was quite spectacular from this vantage point.

We took turns at manning the lines, of which there were three. During my turn I was a little afraid that a fish would indeed bite. I was not all that sure that I could handle one, especially anything large.

But no one had any bites at all. Not one. Not even the Mexicans, who were surely superior fishermen (although I do not exactly see how much skill can come into this).

We reached the small rocky island, our destination: a little beach, beyond which was what looked to be impenetrable underbrush—a small island jungle (where now, no doubt, a tawdry high-rise stands), with a small flotilla of boats, going to and from Ixtapa. Our crew brought out sandwiches and beer, all the while assuring us that on the way back we would surely catch some fish, probably all of us would catch at least one.

We reached the gate to our bay, and were passing the

rocks with their trees, and no one had caught anything at all—when I (of all people) felt a great wrench at my pole, and it was clear to everyone, even to me, that I had caught a fish.

The Mexican boys pulled it out for me, and if what I did was truly to be called "catching a fish," I cannot say much for that sport.

The fish was about a foot long and very beautiful, though, with a bright rainbow of scales that dulled very quickly, as he died. We had Ernestina cook him that night, after first taking a great many pictures, each of us with my fish. And that night on the Martins's porch, the six of us had the poor fish as an hors d'oeuvre, a tiny portion for each. Impossible not to think of the biblical loaves and fishes.

And that was our adventure for that year.

A NOTHER YEAR, R. and I decided to check out the restaurant where we had had the first Martin anniversary dinner, on the way to Los Gatos—and the hotel was in the process of being built above it. "Oh, it's going to be extremely beautiful, so elegant," Celeste had told us. "We might even desert Carlos and stay there."

The restaurant and bar were empty when we got there, although it looked as though people had recently been around.

We walked through that area and up some broad stone steps, up and up, at last reaching—total decay, a chaos of torn mattresses, broken plumbing fixtures (stuff that had been rather fancy, once, huge black tubs and stylish bidets), bent and rusted frames. It was picturesque, surreal, if you will, looking out from that disaster to the lovely sea, the beach and the graceful curve of the bay—but also a little frightening, I felt; soon the encroaching jungle would have devoured it all. And the sight was depressing, as any terrific area of waste is depressing, especially in a country that is so extremely poor.

ON WHAT must have been our twelfth year there, Charles looked very bad indeed, we thought. A very thin man, he was thinner yet, and his pale old eyes were vague, almost unfocused. We even wondered at Celeste's bringing him there, for that is what it amounted to. But we decided that she knew (and loved) him best. She must have known that he could take some pleasure from being there. Or maybe their *not* going to Zihuatanejo, when they always had, would have been even worse for him. In any case, that year Charles hardly left his room, and we saw rather little of Celeste, who was busy with his care and would accept no help.

By this time we had become very close friends, R. and I and the Martins, and so we were intimately involved with his final illness, which began in the spring that followed that January time in Mexico. Also, the hospital to which he eventually came was a couple of blocks from where we lived, and so sometimes Celeste would spend nights with us (they lived somewhat north of San Francisco, in Marin County). We were daily visitors to Charles.

After the death of Charles, which took place in June, Celeste soon became very strangely and intensely involved with an old business friend of theirs, a much younger man, blond, alcoholic, bisexual (nothing against bisexual people: I just very much disliked and distrusted this man). His name (unfortunately) was also Charles; we all called him Chuck. I did not and do not understand the nature of this involvement, I only know that on the part of Celeste, at least, it was a romance, and a highly dramatic one.

She brought him along to Zihuatanejo the following year.

Not only "Chuck," but another friend, a woman of about Celeste's own age, came too, as a sort of duenna, it seemed. Dorothy, tall, once beautiful, generally pleasant but not at all bright, and politically somewhere to the right of Ronald Reagan. She was prepared, it soon came out, not to like Mexico at all—so full of Mexicans, those shiftless wetbacks. It was a very unpropitious situation all around—though not without its comic aspects, if you looked at it with sufficient distance, which I frequently tried and sometimes failed to do. It was all made worse by the fact that Celeste and Dorothy were sharing a room (I cannot imagine why, unless the whole plan was concocted at the very last minute and only one room was available). Fortunately for us, they were not in the Martins's old Room 14 but in another room that was some distance from ours.

The first real sign of trouble came one morning on the beach. Celeste came down alone, and quite contrary to her custom, she greeted us with a certain brittle effusiveness, her mind obviously elsewhere. She even sat down with us, in our *palapa*. And then she told us, as though it were unimportant, that Chuck and Dorothy had gone into town for some shopping.

Inanely—this seemed to call for inanity—we said we hoped that they liked Zihuatanejo.

"It's very hard on Chuck, he's allergic to the sun," Celeste confided. "But he thinks it's so beautiful. And I thought a rest would do him good."

Next, somewhat after noon, teetering across the beach in her high-heeled sandals came tall, giggling Dorothy. And after her, red-faced (perhaps from his allergy), came Chuck, grinning like a sheep. They had found the most darling bar, a real discovery, they told everyone within earshot. We must all go there soon for cocktails. But for the moment, lunchtime, they really weren't hungry at all, they had headaches, needed to get out of the sun. This shift in tone may have been caused by the face of Celeste, which was fiercely disdainful.

We took Celeste to lunch that day at Elvira's. She did not exactly discuss the situation, only saying, "You know Dorothy hasn't had any male attention since Holton died, and I think she's a little starved," and she gave a terrible laugh. I think she was suffering badly.

THAT YEAR, too, there were more cruise ships than ever before. We would wake in the mornings to see something white and enormous, anchored out there in the bay, and we would watch as lifeboats were lowered and passengers clambered down into the boats and headed over to the little town. To saturate it with their purchasing power, to color it up with their gaudy cruise clothes.

Worse, groups in large boats from these cruise ships would come over to our beach for highly organized games of volleyball, and lunch. People we knew who were staying in another hotel down the beach thought it was fun to line up for lunch with the boat folk. "A really free lunch," they told us. We did not think it looked like fun at all.

AT SOME point during that year's visit we were told that poor handsome Arnaldo had gone on a drunken spree in the jungle near his restaurant, the Capricio—that he had shot off a gun into the air. The police were called to subdue him and in doing so, shot him dead. A most horrible, most Mexican story, we thought.

THAT YEAR there were no cats at all in the dining room. No cats anywhere around. This is something that I did not want to think about, and so I did not ask. Not wanting to be told.

BACK IN San Francisco, Celeste continued to see "Chuck," although there were melodramatic intervals of "breaking up." Of anger and recriminations, I think mostly to do with his drinking.

And then Celeste got very sick, and in a couple of weeks she died. Although she had indeed been extremely sick with the cancer that had finally returned, it still seemed (to me) a willed death. I felt (perhaps irrationally) that she could have stayed around a little longer if she had wanted to. (I may have only felt that because I so loved her and wanted her to live forever.) But I think she was tired of being old and alone, although she was beautiful still and lived in a beautiful house. She was lonely for Charles, and tired of Chuck, who did not behave well at all in her illness (there was an ugly story to the effect that he had promised to come to see her the night she died and did not).

And later, as I have said, R. and I broke up, after all that time. Most wretchedly.

And so I do not go back to Zihuatanejo anymore.

I know people who do, however, and they all tell me that it is quite unchanged, which is what I would like to think.

CHAPTER
FOUR

BAJA CALIFORNIA

S INCE I felt that I could no longer go to Zihua-tanejo—general busyness was involved, along with reasons of sentiment (missing R.)—for several years I did not go to Mexico at all, but each January, when I was *supposed* to have been in Zihuatanejo, I felt an awful lack, and in fact, during both those Mexico-less Januaries I succumbed to bad cases of flu; it occurred to me that I might be literally sick with longing for that annual trip, for warmth and flowers, for *bolillos* and garlicky seafood, for the smell of Mexico. In any case, it was clearly time to go back.

Baja California began to seem more and more the right choice. For various reasons. First, I had never been there and knew that I needed a new place. Second, Baja had been the original alternative to Zihuatanejo, before I was so seduced by the horrible F.'s and their compelling aversion to Z. Also, flying down to anywhere in Mexico from California, one passes over that long spiny strip, a ridged desert, mostly, with here and there sparse lines of roads, a few narrow beaches—with the brilliant blue sea on either side. Baja, then, is often what one first sees of Mexico from the air, a further reason for making it my port of reentry, so to speak.

A painter friend, Fred, said that he would like to come along—for all the obvious reasons (first because they simply see so much) I enjoy traveling with painters and other visual types (including some writers).

Fred, though, had once spent some time in the Yucatán, where he had had very bad experiences of two sorts. First, and not too surprisingly, since his stomach is "delicate," he got very sick; according to Fred, this lasted for weeks, with after-effects continuing even back in San Francisco. Second, and really far worse, was an incident in which he and his traveling pal of that time were set upon by some Mexican teenage punks, who threw beer cans at them, shouting, "Queers go home! Lousy American fags, out of Mexico!" Horrible, and terrifying. Though Fred and his friend were uninjured, they were thrown into panic which, along with the *turista,* lasted long after their trip was over.

I tried to persuade Fred that I did not think he would have such experiences in Baja. "They've got to be more used to Americans, all kinds of Americans. Gay people surely go down to Baja," I argued (hoping this to be the case).

And then Fred himself, really wanting to go along, developed the somewhat curious theory that since Baja was not exactly mainland Mexico, the food would be okay.

And how I hoped that we both were right—as we made our reservations for a week in Cabo San Lucas, in March.

It would seem a simple matter, when one looks at a map, to get from San Francisco to Baja California, but of course it is not simple, and that trip with Fred, as has been true of so many voyagings to Mexico, was both difficult and complex.

W E W E R E to fly from San Francisco to Los Angeles in the early afternoon and there make a connection for Cabo San Lucas. This was to involve a change of airlines, and to make the whole venture more festive, we booked into first

class, in the L.A.-to-Cabo stretch (there was some sort of
promotional bargain offer involved). An eminently civilized
plan, we thought, as we looked forward to our first-class
dinner, high up in the Mexican skies.

The first snag was a long delay in the San Francisco
airport: high winds. We sat in our plane and fumed and
worried about making the connection. And, at last arrived in
L.A., we had considerable trouble finding the location of the
second airline; some people had never heard of it, and those
who had gave us conflicting directions, as we puffed along
with our bags (we had checked nothing through; I have had
some experience with the deflection of luggage from Mexico).

When we did find our airline, at last, and the proper
waiting room for the flight to Mexico, we were told that the
plane was an hour late, bad weather in Florida having delayed
it there.

Instead of leaving at 7:00, we would leave at 8:00.

And then it would leave at 8:30, at 9:00, 9:30. By 9:30 I
was hungry and insisted on getting a sandwich; Fred, holding
out for the first-class dinner, had a cup of decaf.

The plane finally took off at about 10:30. There were six
people in first class: us, and ahead of and behind us, two
couples of semiattractive young men, in whom the stewardess
was very interested, very turned on by all four of them. Our
"first-class dinner" was a cold plate of green-spotted (really)
roast beef and some runny potato salad, served with a glass of
California jug wine. So much for our expectations of grandeur, our extravagant greed. (And I do hope that airline really
fails, as most recent word suggests that it will.) I was thinking,
of course, of earlier trips to Z., on Mexican airlines: what fun
they were, how festive.

The airport in Cabo San Lucas is modest. We disem
barked with a minimum of fuss and walked through the building and out into the thick, black, star-studded Mexican night,

where at first there seemed to be no cabs. However, an official-seeming man informed us that there soon would be a bus, which would take us all to our hotel. (For some reason I found this more reassuring than Fred did; he kept looking about rather wildly, muttering that we must rent a car.)

Perhaps half an hour later we indeed were in a van, with the requisite eight other people, its complement. And we headed out into the night, into the familiar smells of dust and dung and flowers, and distantly the sea, that to me mean Mexico. We passed the clusters of familiar shacks, the floorless, open hovels of the extremely poor, those omnipresent hundreds of thousands, the millions of marginal lives, adjacent to our own.

The van ride took quite a while. One couple was dropped off at a hotel, and then another, and then the van turned off the highway and onto an impossibly stone-cobbled road, not fit for cars at all and barely lit. On and on we jolted (Fred and I whispered to each other, laughing, "Ah, this is obviously ours"), until we reached some buildings that were large and dark and ominous. The van stopped at a sort of outdoor desk: We got out and said our names, and indeed it was our hotel, we were expected there. In Building C.

At that moment a very small, very bent man mysteriously appeared, bearing a precariously slanted tray of margaritas in long-stemmed plastic glasses. The very last thing we wanted, just then, but we liked the gesture—so welcoming, so festive. We took the proffered glasses, indeed we took them with us into the car to which we were directed, as we heard the driver exclaim, *"Casa C? Ah, Jesús!"*

And Casa C was indeed a long, even bumpier ride away from the main building. We saw what the driver meant, as again we jolted along, spilling margaritas all over ourselves.

Having asked for separate rooms, we seemed to have been given separate suites—both Fred and I could have brought along whole retinues of friends. This was not entirely clear until the morning, though; that night, as I settled into my room (one of my rooms), the first thing that I really saw was the view from the long French doors: rocks and a crashing surf, so romantically beautiful that I thought, as I so often had on trips to Mexico, that the whole boring, tiresome trip had been more than worth it, I would do it again in a minute, anytime.

And I wondered: Is that not quite possibly an important part of my addiction to Mexico? I *like* the ultimate sense of great vicissitudes finally overcome.

The next morning Fred and I somehow found each other; in all that vast space that we inhabited—and more remarkably we found the dining room, across a complicated area of lawns and pools and paths, an area in which frequently, over the next few days, we got lost.

At breakfast, we saw that most of the other guests were Americans, mostly in family groups; they had the look of people who liked it there, who would come to this same place year after year. People in pastel sports clothes and fishing hats. With many small children. They all seemed very much at home, they were not at all like people in a foreign country. I saw none of the slightly defiant and/or slightly embarrassed stance that one often observes on Americans abroad. And of course, for North Americans Mexico is neither "abroad" nor (so we delude ourselves) genuinely foreign. Baja California, especially, seems still a part of California—despite its melo-dramatically Spanish history.

B LACK PEARLS are what first drew the conquering Spanish to this region; also, according to some accounts, Cortés confused the territory that is now Baja with a mythical island called Calafia—said, in sixteenth-century legend, to be ruled by the queen of the Amazons. He sent various expeditions to Baja, which were all beset by more than the usual number of horrendous vicissitudes: mutinies, attacks by local Indians (who after all did own the land, and the pearls), and raids by fierce English pirates. Cortés managed to establish a colony there, called Santa Cruz, but this did not last long, falling prey both to Indian raids and to disease (the Indians were, of course, especially vulnerable to illnesses imported by the Spaniards, from minor diseases like measles to smallpox and TB).

Jesuit priests controlled Baja for most of the seventeenth century, to be replaced by Father Junípero Serra, who was later to establish many missions in California. During the Mexican War (1846–48) Baja was occupied by Americans for a year, then ceded to Mexico in the same Treaty of Guadalupe Hidalgo that ceded California to the United States—much against the wishes of many U.S. patriots, who felt that Baja was rightfully ours. Especially one William Walker (a real pre-Contra thinker, from the sound of him), who invaded La Paz in 1853, claiming that Baja was a U.S. territory of which he was president. He did much the same thing in Nicaragua a few years later and ended up before a firing squad.

It is not quite clear what justified this belief in saner people that Baja was really "ours," but perhaps to some extent, albeit half-consciously, it still persists.

The Trans-Peninsular Highway was completed in 1973—a great boon, of course, to the tourism that, along with fishing and agriculture, is the area's major industry. There is also an extensive *maquiladora* program in Baja, *maquiladoras* being assembly-plant operators whose wages (80¢ an hour, in 1988) are almost double the average wages elsewhere in Mexico. Thus, there is less unemployment in Baja than in other states of Mexico—which is not to say that it is still not an extremely poor area. We all know about the truly invisible poor, at home as well as in Mexico, who live below statistics.

A FTER BREAKFAST we took a van into the town in Cabo San Lucas, along with a very pleasant, attractive young couple from Dallas, who had come for the fishing. And the young woman told us a curious story—illustrative, I guess she thought, of the Mexican character (about which nearly all Texans are experts, just as many Southerners used to insist that they were able to tell you what Negroes are "really like"). She and her husband had gone fishing the day before, "with this really mean old guy, but he owned the boat." And they caught this marlin, "just a little old biddy one, not any good." The Texans wanted to throw it back: "We're *sports* fishermen, we don't do it for game." But the mean boat owner just clobbered that poor little fish right there, on its head. "Can you imagine?" What I did imagine was that maybe the boat owner's wife would throw that small dead marlin into a pot of fish soup, or so I hoped. But I could have been quite wrong, and maybe the man was just as the Texas lady said, a mean old guy.

Texans are indeed odd about Mexicans, and Mexico, in my experience. A friend of mine, a man of exceptional intelligence, generosity, and other great virtues, a Texan, has been several times heard to say, "If you ever see a photograph of me in Mexico, you will know that my plane has been hijacked." (It's better in his Bay City accent.)

B AJA HAS the world's largest variety of cactus and even if one did not know that fact, it would be apparent that cactus exists there in many, many shapes and shades of green to greenish-yellow—bearing, variously, both prickles and flowers. The terrain of that particular area, near Cabo San Lucas, is desert country: hardened, crevassed, pale coarse sand, and at the time of that particular visit, early March, it was sprinkled here and there with tiny desert wildflowers, pink, purple, and yellow, with many shades in between. And rocks: wild, sculptured outcroppings here and there of boulders, and the sea in most places along that coast is bound with rocks, the beaches are sparse and small. This is primarily fishing or hunting country—a sports rather than a beach resort.

Mexican skies have always looked larger to me than any other skies, and the forms of clouds more various, and more strange. And here again, in Baja, I had this sense of a particularly, peculiarly Mexican sky, with the widest sweep of blue and the oddest small clouds—small clouds that quickly changed to giants and darkened. The quick changes of weather and temperature in Baja are quite remarkable: Within minutes the balmy air can chill your bones, and a fierce mean wind can replace the gently wafting breeze.

The town of Cabo San Lucas looked almost familiar to me, which is to say that it looked a lot like some other small Mexican towns, with its recently paved main streets and on either side the upraised, open, rather garish shops for tourists. And a block away the unpaved, muddy streets, livestock running about amid the shanty dwellings of the very poor, the native Mexicans. In Cabo San Lucas, the harbor is off to one side, with its very heterogeneous collection of shabby fishing boats and the larger, brighter boats of visiting foreigners, sport fishers from Texas and points north and west.

S HOPPING: MEXICO still induces a sort of feeding frenzy in tourist shoppers. The plethora and in most cases the prettiness of silver jewelry especially, but also of leather belts and bags, woven baskets, rebozos, hand-carved animals, and tiles—all this provokes a state of dizzy greed. So many silver earrings for less than ten dollars, for less than twenty— so that if you buy a ring, say, for thirty-five, it seems a major purchase. (My own favorite rings that I wear all the time are opals; I bought them on the beach at Zihuatanejo, along with one from Laredo, for about ten dollars each, and they are very beautiful, I think, although I do not expect them to last my lifetime.) In Baja, shopping is easier than elsewhere in Mexico because it is mostly done in dollars—you don't have to make all those confusing transpositions, the thousands of pesos into far fewer dollars. Fred and I never changed any money on this trip, making all our transactions in hard American cash.

One has to exercise some restraint, finally; it would be a little silly, after all, to buy Christmas presents for everyone for years to come *right now*. Besides, you might come back to Mexico and find even more beautiful bargains.

O N PRINCIPLE, we had dinner each night in a different new hotel, those highly financed Fonatur (the Mexican tourist agency) ventures. There was one that was especially beautiful, we thought: an open terrace from which a garden of sand and cactus plantings extended to the edge of the cliff, above the sea—but the effect was more Japanese than Mexican. On the night we were there a lovely, very elusive orange-striped cat glided in and out among the tables, avoiding overly friendly gringos like us, not straying too far from the kitchen.

Another hotel, very attractive, and the one with the best margaritas, we decided, had an entirely Beverly Hills sort of prettiness, presumably so that certain Californians would feel at home; though in that case, one obviously asks, why come to Mexico?

One particular hotel strongly drew us, since we saw from its location on the map that it faced the Pacific side of Baja, reputed to be extremely dangerous: Each year several people drown at that beach—one hears of people just walking along the sand, to be seized by giant waves and pulled out and down into the surf, then lost. We would go to that particular hotel for lunch, we decided, for lunch and a walk on the beach—at a very safe distance from those waves, the sea.

First the walk. We went up through the hotel grounds, the cluster of small pools and winding paths that led past rather-too-open guest rooms, we thought, but the guests there seemed not to mind and stared out at us quite pleasantly, as we stared back. We were part of their scenery, I guess. We were, in fact, looking for some access to the beach, imagining that surely there must be such: surely a clearly marked path, or a definite flight of stairs somewhere?

What we did find at last were some stairs so broken, so abandoned-looking, that we still thought there must be another way; there it was, however, and there we were, and so we clambered down a steep cliff of sand, on wooden slats that were often broken or missing. At the bottom we simply jumped off, and down onto the beach.

We walked in a direction that seemed to be south, toward the farthest, southernmost tip of Baja, the end of that world. And I thought of the end of another world, that rocky, jutting, wind-torn edge of Portugal, the westernmost tip of Europe, at Sagres, where Henry the Navigator had his school for sailors, from whence Vasco da Gama set out to round, at last, Cape Horn.

To our right as we hiked along was the sea; to our left was what looked to be a housing development, all white and somewhat "Moorish" in style. People were walking around there, either looking to buy or actually moving in. How very frustrating it would be, I thought, to live on a beautiful beach and face an ocean in which you could never swim. These people must be very dedicated sport fishers indeed.

The sea that day did not look particularly dangerous. Only the fact that it was absolutely bare of bathers, runners, or sunbathers, suggested that this was not what it looked to be, not just a broad, coarse-sanded, sunny beach. Out in the ocean a few small boats moved along, motor-powered fishing craft.

Ahead of us, then, we began to see rocks, large outcroppings, a large pale cliff of rocks, and this seemed a proper destination for us. We would walk as far as the rocks, we said. But what we arrived at, finally, was more spectacular, far more amazing than any mere rocks that either of us had ever seen.

There was a wall of granite, maybe thirty feet high, of a soft sand color, and all eroded, quite unevenly, as though intricately, marvelously carved. It looked indeed very much like the façades of some Mexican churches, those long, strange figures of saints, in the style loosely called "Churrigueresque." The lines were mostly vertical, but still, illusory faces appeared here and there, and limbs. And sometimes caves. And real flowers, those tiny, stronger-than-anything, bright survivors, apparently self-nourishing, peering up from their high purchases, their darkened crannies.

Immediately before us were more rocks, in stranger shapes, a true sculpture garden. ("A lexicon of rocks," Fred said.) More granite, some of it pink, with here and there veins of quartz. In Noguchi or Matisse shapes.

These were fascinating rocks. Quite thrilling.

We stood there transfixed, saying (tritely, helplessly), "How come we don't have a camera?" or (for Fred) "a sketchbook?"

Later on, in San Francisco, we talked to friends about those rocks and found that we were hardly the only people so attracted: "Oh, *those* rocks," we heard from various people who had seen them, including several local artists. And we found another couple who had actually climbed up and all over our rocks. (Interesting, this difference in response to the rocks, proving Fred's point: It was indeed a lexicon, to be read as one would.)

Reluctantly, we headed at last back and up to the hotel and found that going up those broken stairs was a lot harder than going down. But we made it, and having wandered through the fairly quiet hotel again, we came to a nice sunny terrace where lunch was being served. A small table of teenage Texas girls, all pretty but a little shrill, was at our left. No one else. Just up some steps from our terrace was a bar with seats near the edge and a view no doubt superior to our own.

We were settling into our guacamole, beers, whatever, when sudden shouts began, from all over, and as is the case with group hysteria, it was some moments before we could get any idea of what had happened. At first everyone was simply shouting and running about. Then we learned that a man had fallen from the cliff. At first believing that the railing of the bar above was meant, I further imagined a drunken suicide; it did seem an odd time and place and circumstance in which to take one's life, and I thought, Was he terribly drunk? Quarreling with his wife or girlfriend at the bar?

It then became known that the man had fallen from somewhere else, and I instantly thought of the stairs, though it was hard to envision severe injury, just from falling down into sand.

By this time the waiters and busboys and what were presumably managers were rushing through our terrace, and it had been ascertained that the man had fallen from a lookout point just below where we were.

"There's no way he could survive that fall," said a tearful Texas adolescent.

In that case, why was so much ice being carried down to the beach? I hoped it was not to preserve the corpse.

We heard the siren of what turned out to be the ambulance, and as we looked down to the beach there it was, heading toward the spot where the man had fallen, an area now so crowded with people that it was impossible to tell what was going on. The ambulance, because of deep sand, I guess, had stopped some distance away, and as we watched, four attendants trudged forward. We continued to watch as, bearing a stretcher with a sheet to hold up over it for protection from the sun, they marched back to the waiting ambulance.

THE MAN who fell not only survived, he did not even break anything.

We found that out at dinner, news of that nature seeming to travel fast. And Fred and I acknowledged to each other that we had somehow always believed in his survival, we had not got caught up in the general lunchtime hysteria out of that conviction—and not from hardheartedness, as the Texas girls may well have suspected.

We were having that meal, our last, in our own hotel, in the outside portion of our dining room, where the view was much like that from my suite: rocks and crashing waves, and on that particular night, a glittering, moonlit sea.

"I'd really like to come back and see those rocks again," Fred told me, and I agreed that I would too, very much. For us, too, they had become "those rocks."

"Besides, everyone spoke to me here," Fred continued.

"But, Fred—"

"I mean it. They see me with you, and they think we're a couple, and they're all so terrifically friendly. If I were with Bill, no one would speak. No one ever does, when we travel."

"You don't think it's because you two guys seem so private? Even a little severe?" (This is quite true, they do; I would hestitate to speak, if we hadn't met.)

"*No,* I don't think that. It's been like that all my life. You really can't imagine."

And I suppose he is right, that I can't imagine.

In any case, Fred and I, in San Francisco, are still discussing this point, trying to avoid words like *paranoia* and *homophobia.*

I am glad, though, that his experience in Baja was so generally good and that we can also discuss a return trip.

I HAVE noticed, in fact, that I have a very strong tendency to want to plan trips back to a place I've just left. I used to travel a lot with a man (R., in fact,) who found this especially crazy. Why on earth come back from Sicily, he said, and start right in talking about more Sicily, adding Agrigento and Siracusa to the trip? I can see what he meant, I guess; for me, however, this habit of mind is like my tendency to want more and more of a writer whose book I have just finished. Wanting all, in fact, of Trollope. Of Iris Murdoch. Of Joyce Carol Oates.

In any case, then and there I began to think about where I would like next to go in Baja.

CHAPTER
FIVE

SAN MIGUEL DE ALLENDE

SAN MIGUEL, north of Mexico City, is quite simply one of the prettiest towns I've ever seen. (Pretty: To me, San Francisco and San Miguel are pretty; Paris and Venice are beautiful.) A hill town, it affords everywhere lovely views of rooftops and distant mountains, of narrow cobbled streets and tree-lined little squares—and churches, everywhere churches. Perched in the Bajío, the most Catholic center of colonial Mexico, San Miguel abounds in churches, all interesting and many quite beautiful. The main church, generally called the *parroquia* (parish church), dominates the landscape with its cluster of lacy spires around a taller, still lacier spire. This church, reputedly designed by an "ignorant" (this means Indian) stonemason who was inspired by postcards of Gothic churches, has somewhat the look of Gaudí's Sagrada Familia, the church in Barcelona, another "ignorant" work.

From wherever you are in San Miguel, you can see those mildly crazy-looking towers, and if your hotel is near that church, that central square, you can always get your bearings and make it home.

But everywhere you look affords some pleasure: here an intricate wrought-iron balcony overflowing with dark pink bougainvillea; there a carved stone cornice, wildly decorative, the somber face of a saint embedded in flowers; and there a long curved wall of the reddish brick-dust color that is highly characteristic of San Miguel (I heard it afterwards described as a pink city, but that is both inaccurate and misleading); a wall topped by thick, green, tumbling, tangled vines. And then another view, down a narrow street that seems to drop off in a vista of far-off green mountains, and sky, and clouds.

ONCE MORE, though, as with most Mexican trips, getting to San Miguel posed certain problems (although on the map and in tourist guides it is very easy). I flew to Mexico City from San Francisco easily enough, and there Rosemary, a sometime painter, sometime architect, with whom I had traveled to Zihuatanejo, came to meet me. She had heard that the train from Mexico City to San Miguel was a very great treat, and it left at 7:30 A.M., she said. I was very unenthusiastic about such an early start, getting up at 6:00 and all that running about, but I agreed to go along. However, the travel agent at our hotel informed us that the time had since been changed to 7:00; we would have to be at the station at 6:00, and even then we could not be sure of tickets. And so, to my considerable relief, that was out (Rosemary is generally a much better sport, a more relaxed traveler than I am). The concierge next told us that first-class buses leave every hour for San Miguel. A tiny inner voice informed me that this was unlikely, the voice that is always accurate and to which one too often does not listen.

We got to the bus station at about 10:20 the next morning, feeling that we were in plenty of time for the first-class bus at 11:00. But there was no first-class bus at 11:00, there was no first-class bus until 2:30, we were firmly told; however, if we hurried a great deal, we could make the second-class bus at

10:30. Which we did, running along the platform with our bags, probably looking even sillier than we thought we did.

Since the two days on a second-class bus going from Puerto Escondido to Zihuatanejo with Rosemary and her husband, Paul, I have thought that perhaps second-class travel is included in the karma of our friendship. In any case, this trip, especially as compared to that earlier trip, was quite all right: a fairly clean and not too crowded bus. A lot of stops, but we still made fairly good time.

Once the bus stopped for a man who turned out to be selling a painkilling salve; he went on and on about its wonders, as the bus drove northward, toward the green mountains, and several people bought his salve. While out to our left, going in the direction opposite to ours, toward Mexico City, there was an enormous procession, thousands of people, men and women, bearing religious banners—pilgrims, on their way to some shrine. For an hour or so then it rained, on all the fields and plains, on the mountains ahead, and on all the long massed lines of pilgrims.

It was still raining when we got to San Miguel, where we piled into the pickup truck that seemed to be the town's lone taxi. We drove up, and up, up a maze of those narrow cobbled streets, of which we could see very little, but the houses there looked small, and poor—a nontourist area.

Our hotel had been billed as a remodeled eighteenth-century hacienda, as are so many hotels and restaurants in northern Mexico. There was a central, open courtyard, at least two stories high, a feature common to these buildings, and, in the case of our hotel, a lovely atrium of trees and vines, and hummingbirds. There was even a hummingbird nest, as we discovered at breakfast a few days later.

My room was a couple of flights of stairs above all this, atop the main building, it seemed, and although I had been cautioned by San Francisco friends *not* to accept a room in the main building (wisely, as things turned out), I fell in love with this room on sight: It was up a few steps from the large brick patio on which there were pots of flowers, a few lines of billowing laundry, and also had a balcony of its own off to one side, with a table and chairs and a marvelous view of everything—cathedral spires and rooftops, streets and hills of houses, and a distance of blue-green mountains.

Also, as I approached the room on that first day, on my own front steps there was a nice, small, shy, black cat, who turned out to have two small kittens, a gray and a black one, in the woodshed next to the steps. These days I have a firm rule against emotional involvements with animals met on trips, but I did like this cat, who looked much like a younger version of one of the cats I had left at home, named Black. And I loved her kittens, who were attempting their first weak-kneed tottering out onto the bricks, like drunks in strong sunlight; they were happier scrambling about in the woodpile, their own dark bar. From our separate forms of distrust we kept our distance from one another, those cats and I—although on several nights I did bring up scraps from dinner, and the mother watched as her babies bolted bits of fish.

I HAD briefly visited San Miguel about twenty years back, with R. We stayed in a nice place out of town from which we walked in, and looked about, and then left—too soon. Typically, I had wanted to come back, I had been so taken with its prettiness, but in the intervening years I had heard a great deal about what sounded like an extreme case of Americanization. If you mention San Miguel in San Francisco, everyone seems to know people who have retired there, or gone off there to write or paint or study languages (or to study equitation; that, too, is possible in San Miguel—there are famous horses). Or all of those. And so I imagined a population of students and semirich, quasi-artistic retirees. And I turned out to be not so very far wrong, though in a more limited sense than I had imagined. And the limitation is curiously geographic: All around the Plaza Alende, the pretty tree-lined park that faces the *parroquia,* a square that is known as the *jardín,* tourists, students, and American residents circulate, in and out of the long arcades of stores, the tourist office, the small restaurants of that area. But a couple of blocks away, in the Plaza San Francisco, fronted by the façades of two small and very beautiful churches, one sees only Mexicans. And a few blocks from there you come to the open market, which is apparently in operation all day every day· There are fruits and vegetables and tortillas, cooked bits of pork or fish that smell most wonderful but are sure to be lethal to foreigners, or so we are led to believe. In any case, you do not see a lot of tourists in those markets, maybe a few stray students here and there. Just beyond the market—in fact, the market seems to spill over onto its grounds—is the strange and beautiful façade of the church of St. Philip Neri (according to a priest whom we met later on, and spent some time with, Neri was the founder of opera, as we know it—among other things). The arched carved wooden door is flanked by long pilasters and recessed, elongated figures of saints, and on either side is a large panel of the local brick-colored plaster.

On one side of the building is a high white bell tower, its three tiers of bells topped by a tiny, somewhat incongruous weather vane. That tower, though in its way quite lovely, still gives the whole that slightly lopsided, mildly deranged look that Mexican churches so often have; they were clearly made by striving, imperfect, talented, but fallible humans (mostly Indian workers, which does rather give the lie to the myth of their laziness), which may account for some of their strong appeal.· Certainly the Mexicans who live around these churches feel "at home" in them; the churches are always in use, in one way or another. You never enter an empty church. And the worshipers, while deeply reverent (sometimes a little hysterically so; I remember a man wildly waving his hands at a statue of the virgin, in the *parroquia*), are not awestruck. It is as though they worshiped familiars, and indeed the figures of the bleeding Christ, and Christ flagellated, are all too human. It is human anguish and literal blood that are portrayed.

And you do not see (or *I* did not see) a lot of Americans wandering through these churches, and heaven knows not worshiping there. (There is an active local Episcopal church, a small, discreetly unornamented building.) In all my wanderings in and out of San Miguel's many churches, I was almost always the only gringo in the room.

The Americans, then, seem to cluster in their own places. On our first night in San Miguel, Rosemary and I went to a restaurant that had looked appealing on our stroll about the town that afternoon—a narrow, open, vine-sheltered interior space. By nighttime, about eight, which is, of course, very early by Mexican standards, it was packed with what looked to be students. The oddity was that none of them seemed to know each other, no convivial table-hoppings, no greetings. A week or so later, however, some other Americans who had gone to the same place on their first night reported great conviviality; we must have hit the first night of a new term at the school.

A CENTER of considerable and very worthy North American activity is the American Library, founded in 1954 in a pretty former convent school, with a large central open patio. The library boasts "the largest bilingual collection of any public library in Mexico: 12,000 books in Spanish, 18,000 more in English."

And one of the main fund-raisers is a Sunday-morning tour of haciendas—for which we eagerly signed up.

The first surprise was the number of people attending—a couple of hundred at least (we had somehow imagined a much smaller group) the point being that locals come, too; as in other towns, including San Francisco, curiosity about other people's houses runs high.

At last, after quite a few speeches—from a group of women who among them possessed an amazing variety of American accents, Back Bay to Brooklyn to Illinois—we were all ushered into the oldest buses I have ever seen, and the slowest; they drove much slower than my normal walking pace, I am sure of that.

But at last we arrived at the first hacienda (I now see that the term is very loosely used, rather like *villa* in Italy and the south of France). This house was new, "colonial-style" rather than colonial, and quite incredibly horrible. Smallish rooms all crowded with brand-new junk, bright new silver and copper, an incredible jumble of colors and textures all piled together, and the bright white plaster walls all scrolled and swirled—a rather condescending notion of what is "Mexican," when you come to think of it. Fortunately, the owners were out of sight.

The second "hacienda," quite nearby, was more of the same, although in two distinct ways much worse: one, the place was full of artworks by the owner; and, two, he was there: a small bent man with, I think, the most humorless face I have ever seen, a piratical face, all ego and greed—the author of all that large, pretentious, kitschy art, nudes and sentimental children, statues of animals, life-sized.

The third dwelling, which was back closer in town, near the *jardín* and the *parroquia,* was a vast improvement. An eighteenth-century house, not overly remodeled, although here and there some cutesy "Mexican" touches. (I guess these objects are irresistible, to some, if you live there.) Also, the two owners were present that Sunday morning, sitting in separate rooms, both with tall glasses of booze, both well on their way to getting plastered. In a way you can't blame them; it must be awful to have a bunch of strangers trooping through your house, making silly comments. Still, not being there at all would surely be preferable; they could just have gone to some bar and spent the day there.

Actually, quite a few of the local Americans whom I took to be retirees had that special alcoholic pallor, the hesitant, shaky gait that one sees on very old, very serious drinkers. And their faces, along with the illness, seemed familiar: These are the very rich who follow artists to the artists' beautiful discoveries, to Cagnes-sur-Mer, to most of the Riviera, to Woodstock and Santa Fe, Carmel and Sausalito. Rich old drunks with a mildly artistic bent, somewhere. Open and affable, and fairly soon the most terrific bores. Which is a very good reason for not living in a place that is even faintly billed as artistic, I think.

The fourth hacienda was very good indeed, large and dark and grand, with an especially beautiful patio, topped by bright-blue flower-painted tiles, and with a row of flowerpots lining the roof above. The furniture was dark, mostly Victorian, with a few massively impressive Regency mirrors. The invisible family, we were told, was that of a local doctor, his wife, and seven children.

This last house seemed a surely intentional contrast to the garish, terrible first—which made the house tour highly instructive, the message being, I think: Never try to imitate established styles, and never tamper with what is already there, and already good.

TO OUR surprise, the food in our pretty hotel was very good. Unexpectedly, the chef was French. Also, a classical guitarist was often there, a thin young man with a pure and gentle style, playing lovely Bach, named Arturo. (Both he and the French chef were to figure, though not together, in the final debacle of our relations with that hotel.)

Despite the good food, however, we often went out for dinner, having an urge to see more of the town and its population. One night we chose the dining room of a neighboring hotel, another very pretty former hacienda, about three blocks from ours—very fortunately, as things turned out.

We had a good and fairly long dinner, in the middle of which a very large and indeterminately Southern couple came in and sat at the table next to ours. (I feel that Texans are blamed for almost every unattractive Southern voice or act; let us say that these people were from Georgia.) They were both more than six feet tall and very heavy, and they drank a lot. I heard the woman complain that the vodka hurt her sinuses, and I watched and listened as the proprietor, a very pretty, very assured woman named Alicia, came to their table and explained that the vodka was a standard brand, perhaps some other explanation could be found for her sinus problems.

And then I stopped paying attention to those people.

Rosemary and I were discussing how we would redo that room—among other topics. I said how much I liked the big, heavy-looking, very simply carved chairs. Rosemary agreed— and we both, in whispers, deplored almost everything else in the room, in pleasant unity of taste.

And then we got up to go, as, at the same moment the Georgians got up too, and in the next instant that woman's chair had crashed across the top of my right foot (I was wearing fairly bare sandals).

"Oh, I hope it didn't get you," the Georgians murmured.

"Well actually, it did. My foot."

"Oh, I'm so sorry—" and they vanished, entirely.

But Alicia was immediately there, in time to see my instantly dark-blue foot, high and swollen. And Alicia turned out to be a holistic medical practitioner, who had lived both in Paris and in India during the late sixties and studied in both places, with her former American husband. She put hot compresses on my foot; I have since been told that cold is better (except by one exceptionally smart doctor who said it really did not matter much). She rubbed nice oils into the swelling. The odd part is that my foot never hurt; it was only swollen and discolored for quite a while.

The main problem was that the swelling made my running shoes out of the question, and those were by far the best gear for cobbles, I had found. I was forced to wear my sandals all the time, and their soles were already too thin. (A long time ago I read an article by a very sophisticated traveler, or so she sounded, whose advice was to take along very old, very comfortable shoes on trips: If they wear out, just throw them away, which will leave more room in your suitcase.)

I spent several days, then, hobbling about with my bandaged bad foot, in my coming-apart, frayed sandals—which gave me a somewhat less removed, less rich-tourist sense of myself in San Miguel. I do not mean that I imagined myself transformed into a Mexican working-class woman, but that is what my feet looked like, and when I looked down at them, I felt slightly less foreign, less remote.

BEGGARS: THERE were fewer by far than in Mexico City or, for that matter, these days, than in New York or San Francisco. Still, every day we would pass at least three or four, mostly very old women, huddled into some steps or a doorway, so weighted with black rags, so bent, that it looked as though they might never rise, or even ever move. With great gnarled hands and withered faces and huge black hopeless eyes.

What to do. Rosemary said that in the States she contributed to organizations that help the homeless, the street people; she had worked for such groups and she would rather give to them than directly to people on the street. I do not have a clear plan, in this regard, and so I do a little of both. In Mexico, though, the situation seemed different. It was not at all clear that any organizations were doing anything; the official attitude could well be that Mexico has always had beggars, street people (except that these are not street people, they sleep in a corner, somewhere, we were sure; maybe in some part of a church). And so, more or less as middle-class Mexicans do, we each gave small amounts (or secret large ones) to most of the beggars we passed.

I had a most curious encounter, in that way: I was bending down to hand a painfully twisted woman some money (she was so dark and infinitely wrinkled, although she could have been about my age) when I slipped on something, and I would have fallen to the sidewalk, except that a strong, firm hand was extended to me, restoring my balance. Her hand. I thanked her and dropped the money onto her lap, and then she thanked me, and then back and forth we thanked each other for several minutes. It was almost funny. Almost.

R OSEMARY HAS four daughters and five grandchildren (I think, at last count); quite understandably,
she fell prey to the local shopping fever, and while my foot was
somewhat indisposed I went along, poking around in stores,
sifting through silver, observing ceramics. And I began to
notice that several stores had small, discrete rooms that were
filled with shelves of very porno ceramics: small painted clay
groups of figures engaged in sexual acts. Mostly men with
women, but also wolves and women—and often a leering
devil is the priapic aggressor. They all seemed quite good-
humored, most of the participants were happily smiling, and
some of the groups, replete with helpful or simply deadpan
spectators, were very funny.

To a North American, the minimal fuss that is made over
such highly visible "obscenity" is interesting and even instructive. (Rosemary and I were tempted to mail off a group or two
to Senator Helms, and maybe we should have.)

T HE NEXT day I was able to get back into my runners,
and Rosemary and I began taking longer walks. One
Sunday morning we went out to a leafy, wooded hilltop up on
the outskirts of town, where there was said to be a famous
orchid garden. However, a sign on the wooden door announced CLOSED ON SUNDAYS, and we were about to turn
around and go when the door opened and an elderly, very
small man motioned us inside with an elegant bow, saying that
of course we were most welcome to see the orchids.

We entered and found a romantic stone ruin, broken
walls, some steps that led to nowhere, and a lovely series of

arches, all overgrown with vines and trees. And orchids—everywhere orchids, in various stages of dormancy, some in wonderful bloom, pinks and spotted yellows and deep exotic browns. Among those ruins some very small children played; a mother was tending her fat brown baby, and chickens ran about, distractedly. A perfect "Mexican" scene, I could not help thinking, along with a number of other "perfect" scenes.

On another day we went out to the Instituto Allende, which has the pleasantly disorganized quality of a functioning art school—housed an in eighteenth-century building, a former summer residence.

And we walked over to Benito Juárez Park, a well-maintained and very pretty public area, said by a local guidebook to have been acquired by the city from some local private owners in the days of the revolution, early in this century.

Next to that park is the public washing place, a series of open stone tubs built around a small square, to which women bring great bundles of laundry, balanced on their heads, also managing to herd along small troops of children. The women vigorously set to their washing, then lay the clothes out to dry on an upraised central area. And of course they talk, and talk—exchanging lives, and troubles, and jokes. And remedies, and recipes.

S AN MIGUEL is not only quite close to the exact geographic center of Mexico, it was also historically central, both to the mass conversions of "ignorant Indians" to Catholicism (known as "civilizing the savages" to historians of that day), and to the Spanish lust for silver; in its surrounding mountains the Spaniards discovered and not so systematically pillaged rich veins of this lovely metal. And, perhaps with some logic, San Miguel is crucial, too, in the story of the country's long revolt from Spanish domination and its ultimate freedom from Spain. It was Father Hidalgo of Dolores, a priest from the hacienda class, an intellectual and a freethinker (he was said to have had several mistresses and children) who, along with Don Ignacio de Allende (for whom the town is named), first proclaimed the independence of Mexico in 1810. Hidalgo and Allende were ultimately defeated and executed by the Spaniards; still, they are held to have struck revolutionary sparks, and they remain heros of the revolution, which was finally accomplished in 1821.

San Miguel's neighboring cities of Guanajuato and Querétaro were both involved in the mining of riches (for the Spaniards) and in the political uprisings that led to freedom. Guanajuato is, in fact, of extreme historical importance in Mexico: It was the first city to surrender to the rebellious forces, under the leadership of Hidalgo. The crucial contest took place in the granary, where the royalists holed up and held out as long as they could—until a young miner (his nickname was El Pípila) forced open the huge doors and burst in. Later, the city was recaptured by the defending forces, and Hidalgo was beheaded; his head was displayed high up on this same granary. And Querétaro too is very important: In 1848 the treaty (held infamous by Mexicans) that gave New Mexico and Texas to the United States was signed in Querétaro. And later still, in 1867, it was in Querétaro that poor Maximilian was finally executed. (His wife, Carlotta, had gone back to Italy to beg for funds; it was in Italy, on that venture, that she went entirely mad.) And: The PRI (Party of Institutional Revolution), which has dominated Mexican politics since 1927, was founded in Querétaro. The proximity of those two cities had, in fact, a great deal to do with our choice of San Miguel as a place for a lengthy stay.

Friends at home had told me about a local tourist office that offered excellent tours and had said, "You must get Luz, she's a wonderful guide. Avoid Donald, he's a bore." I was not at all sure how to proceed if we did, in fact, get Donald; we were assigned to Luz, however, and she was indeed a wonderful guide—in a comfortable mini-van with three other passengers.

Guanajuato is a strange, narrow city built into a riverbed. Periodically the river used to overflow and flood the town. A dam was built at last and customarily, at the end of the season of floods, a prisoner from the local jails was "allowed" to open the gates. This horrendous practice was abandoned when one year the chosen prisoner failed to drown and swam to freedom. This story, particularly vivid and terrible, was told by pretty, very serious Luz; it seemed all the more awful since the day of our visit was dark with rain and more threatening clouds. One could all too easily imagine floods in those narrow, winding streets, and drownings.

For many years Guanajuato was the richest town in Mexico and one of the richest cities of the world—all from silver. We first visited an incredibly grand hacienda there, a mine owner's mansion, with acres of splendid gardens, the flowers now all bent down with rain. A Kennedy daughter was sequestered there for a time, Luz told us. The place was in private hands until recently; now it is open as a museum.

These days Guanajuato is clearly not a rich town. Despite the marvelous architecture—the wonderfully carved stone façades of some of the upper-city houses (up above the floods), and the splendid pink Churrigueresque cathedral— there is a brooding, dark sense of ruin, of a city battered by time, and a too-violent history, and floods, and more floods. But because of the ancient and excellent university there, Luz told us, many refugees from the Spanish Civil War, in the late thirties, and from Franco's Spain, were drawn to Guanajuato, and it has the look, very much, of some once-glorious Spanish city—of Toledo, perhaps, or Valladolid.

After walking about the city for a couple of hours, visiting the Cervantes Museum (there is an important local cult of Don Quixote, with yearly festivals and symposiums) and the Teatro Juárez (a wonderful building, with an elegant red-flocked interior), Luz drove us out to the scenes of the crimes, so to speak, and the source of all that vanished money: out to the mines.

Out in the country, we drove along a rutted, narrow road, red clay, high up in the hills above the town.

"What is it that holds up the cathedral of Notre Dame?" Luz suddenly asked us, worriedly seeking some lost word or phrase.

"Flying buttresses," Rosemary told her.

"Ah yes. Exactly that."

I was wondering about a mine with flying buttresses when there it was: an abandoned mine, with enormous stone flying buttresses thrust out and down into the encroaching growth, the thick tall trees, and vines, and flowering bush, a verdant jungle. Behind those buttresses rose the walls of the mine, huge and gray and broken. Spectral. Surreal. And scary: the lesson of Ozymandias.

The surrounding hills were bare and deeply crevassed, mined-out, and beyond those hills lay the tree-dotted stretching plains of central Mexico, and then further blue mountains, beneath the heavily clouded, menacing sky.

We drove then to the area's active mine and watched as a carload of miners emerged from the earth, wiping at blackened faces, reaching for cigarettes. Working for about $3.67 a day.

THE EXCURSION to Querétaro, also (happily) with Luz, was a cheerier day, undoubtedly so in part because of the blithely sunny weather. (I have to admit to an extreme subjectivity to the moods of weather.) We drove through flat, quite prosperous-looking farmland, then through an extremely ugly industrial area, to a lovely small colonial city (to which many Mexican residents have moved since the eighty-five earthquake, Luz told us). Beautiful small squares, with ornate carved fountains and flower-covered kiosks, the white stone of plaster façades of buildings crossed with lacy wrought-iron balconies. And small alleyways, arched over with flowering bougainvillea.

We saw the large and lavish home of Doña Josefa Ortiz, known as *La Corregidora,* who warned Father Hidalgo and Allende that the Spaniards knew of their plot and so (at least temporarily) spared their lives. "You see? She risked all that great house," was the comment of Luz, as she pointed to that broad, impressive, but most unbeautiful façade.

Far more attractive was the local museum, formerly the Municipal Palace, built in 1750—with its arched inner courtyard, all heavily, baroquely carved, and its pretty central fountain.

Rosemary, an occasional painter, was going through the collection rather more slowly than I was, and so I fell into conversation with Harry, another member of our group, from Philadelphia—a very tall, heavy, white-haired man, quite pale (he had mentioned ill health in our van chatter, coming here). A man who seemed to read a lot (there were references, mostly to writers I had not read for a while: Oscar Wilde, Ronald Firbank). Harry traveled whenever he could, he said.

What did I do? Harry wondered.

I lied (I always lie; I know how dangerous it is to announce yourself as a writer). I said that I teach—well, in fact I occasionally do. But what about him? I asked.

Embarrassed, Harry paused, and then said that he was a

priest. (Could he, too, have been lying? It seems unlikely.) He always traveled without a collar, as he put it.

Rosemary came up then, and the three of us discussed the beauty of the building in which we stood and the paucity of talent among local artists.

We both liked Harry, Rosemary and I decided later on. He had an appealing small twist to his mouth, bespeaking both perplexity and amusement.

"Of course he's a priest," said Rosemary. "No one would just say that. And he looks like a priest."

When we got back to our hotel, Rosemary said that she did not feel well, not at all well. Best to skip dinner, she thought, she was sure to be all right the next day. I believed her on all scores, and we agreed to keep in touch by phone— though we could as easily have called across the way, her tower to mine. I decided to have dinner in the dining room (I don't know why, except that I had not been there before, tending to take our occasional lunches out in the patio), a somewhat formal area. In part, I think, I wondered about who else would eat there. But in that I was totally frustrated: No one else sat down in that room until the end of my meal, at about ten o'clock, when an American group came in—a real estate agent and her new-rich Texan clients.

But all during my meal there was Arturo, the lovely guitarist. He sat in the middle of the room (I was at one end), and he played and played as I ate. In a way a preposterous situation, I thought, and so (to change it a little) I initiated conversation. Haltingly: His English was far worse than my Spanish, and he insisted on English. And for a shy and very courteous young man he asked surprisingly personal questions, I thought (perhaps questions recommended in his English textbooks?). He did not ask, What do you do? (for which I was ready) but rather, Do you have children? Yes, one, a

sculptor. Are you married? No. Oh, you are widow? Yes.
(Another lie, but as good an explanation as any.) And then,
more successfully than our talk had been carried on, Arturo
played. More Bach, and some Spanish songs.

The next problem was whether or not to tip Arturo. If we
had not talked I would have tipped him without a thought,
and so I decided (thinking of the Mexican wage) that his needs
were no doubt greater than any delicate scruples of mine. I
tipped him and said that I very much hoped to see him again.

Arturo's melancholy music, or possibly the allusion to
my "widowhood" (it actually felt a little like that) had sad-
dened me a little, so that I gave, that night, some thought to
traveling alone and to solitude in general—for the most part
unproductive thoughts, and in any case I was not, then, traveling alone; I was with a valued old friend. But I watched with
some envy as two young women in walking shorts, with
backpacks, walked through the patio, looking in at me as I
looked out at them. I wished that I had not chosen the inner
dining room.

The next morning Rosemary said that she still did not
feel well; she was ordering tea in her room, but she would be
all well by afternoon—she could tell.

Down in the patio, as I began my own breakfast, the two
backpack women walked in and, amazingly, it turned out that
we knew one another: They owned and ran a bookstore in
New York, and we had met there. Jill and Jenny. I would have
been glad to see them anywhere but especially then and there.
They ordered coffee, and the three of us began to exchange
travel information. They had just been to a new resort near the
Guatemalan border at which people were drowning in
alarming numbers—you must never go there, they said.

I told them about Luz, and the good trips to Guanajuato
and Querétaro. And they told me about a church that was just

outside of town and that was, they said, the center of a flagellation cult. They had a car: Would I like to go out there later this afternoon?

I would, I would like to very much.

By late afternoon, Rosemary was indeed all well, but Jenny was sick, and so Jill, Rosemary, and I drove out to Atotonilco.

Turning off the main highway, driving slowly along a white dirt road, we soon saw that we had arrived at some sort of festival; to me it looked a little like the county fairs of my North Carolina childhood: people all over, children and animals, and shabby concession booths. Walking along, we began to see some high white plaster walls, scalloped along the top, clearly the walls of the churchyard. And both those walls and the church itself had a Moorish, perhaps North African look, the church with its rounded towers, its small Byzantine apertures.

Immediately in front of the church the final touches were being put to a long piece of latticework, on poles, some of the lattices in the shapes of crosses, and onto the crosses were fastened various homely objects: loaves of bread, and Coke bottles, and flowers. The whole structure must have been intended for a later parade, to be carried aloft, and then (it seems probable) to be burned in a great high pyre.

More crowds thronged the steps of the church, and then the church's interior, which was heavy with the dense sweet smell of tuberoses, of incense, and of many, many bodies.

But nowhere, to our disappointment, did we find any visible signs of flagellation, though that, of course, is what we were looking for. I am not at all sure what we can have expected, though: rows of whips? In any case, not there.

The church itself was densely crowded with objects: statuary and pictures. There was an extremely graphic, bloody picture of Christ being flagellated—but there are many such pictures, all over Mexico, in churches.

"FLAGELLATION IS generally discouraged these days by the church." Harry the priest told us this a few days later, over lunch; we had run into each other accidentally, near the *jardín,* and moved on to lunch. "It is only recommended in cases of extreme remorse. I myself, once or twice, very early," Harry muttered.

But what could he have done? we wondered. Were there special sins among priests, sins other than the ones that come immediately to mind?

Harry lowered his voice. "It can lead to sexual excitement in some people," he told us. "Flagellation."

We said that we had heard of that.

Harry knew nothing about Atotonilco and had heard of no cult of flagellation there. "Although I believe that such a thing exists in New Mexico," he said.

Later he told us something of his life. The youngest of a working-class family of nine, he took orders, as did his youngest sister. He earned about four hundred dollars a month, plus room and board, and still he managed to save and travel. Ireland, Italy, and Mexico were his favorites. We insisted on paying for his lunch, which at first embarrassed him. "People tend to think they have to pay for priests," he said.

"But we're not even Catholics," we told him. "We don't think we have to." He seemed to find that reassuring.

Rosemary, who was just back from Nicaragua, asked Harry what he thought of Liberation Theology and, in general, of the position of the church in Central America. Harry said he knew very little about it; he had heard of Liberation

Theology and meant to look into it. We said that we hoped he did.

When he died, Harry told us, he wanted "Send in the Clowns" to be played at his funeral. Poor Harry: I wonder if that will happen.

HARRY'S HOTEL cost him sixteen dollars a day, he had told us. Ours cost about a hundred apiece—a fact that made us wonder about our choice, since Harry's hotel, from the outside at least, looked perfectly okay, even pretty. We wondered if we were paying all that extra money for the French chef. He was good but hardly worth all that, and besides, we hardly ever ate there. God knows neither Rosemary nor I is especially fond of expensive hotels per se; on the contrary, the very fact of paying a lot of money can make a person cross. Once in New York, for no very good reason (I suppose I was proving something to myself), I stayed in a terribly expensive hotel, all remodeled into fake old-English, and I hated my room, which looked like a study into which a bed had been arbitrarily injected, and I became very annoyed over the fact that a shoeshine cost $2.50.

Our rooms in San Miguel were indeed very beautiful, however, especially their views, and so far they were very quiet—and at noon and at night, as we walked through the patio, there was Arturo with his guitar, the sounds of Bach filtered through Segovia. All of which is to say that we were in no way prepared for the eruption of Bastille Day.

For several days there had been a small sign posted near the front door announcing the arrival of a famous accordionist from Paris—for a special Bastille Day celebration. To all of which we paid very little attention, although I did think, Oh dear, I hope he doesn't interfere with Arturo.

But: We got back from dinner one night, the night of July 14, at about ten o'clock, to find our quiet, pretty patio overwhelmed with noise and festivity. There, indeed, was the accordionist, a wild-haired punk type, with a huge amplifier. Small *tricolore* flags were stuck all over the place. Even the waiters, above their dark, stern faces, wore funny French party hats. And every table overflowed with festive singing, shouting guests, also in paper hats. *In Mexico*

Mounting the stairs to my room, I was quite clearly aware of several facts: One, this party would go on and on, into the night. And two, there would be absolutely no point in protesting; it would not only be pointless but lacking in style. To protest a successful party would make it clear that one was a lonely, crotchety spoilsport, which is exactly what I felt like.

Certainly I was right in my first premise: The music went on and on, all night (or so it seemed to me, as I tried to read). I was reading the marvelous account of early travels in Mexico by Frances Calderón de la Barca, a wonderfully witty and observant Scottish lady whose husband was the first ambassador to free Mexico from Spain, in the mid-nineteenth century. Unfortunately, that night I came to her observations on flagellation:

> I felt rather frightened, and would have been very glad to leave the church, but it would have been impossible in the darkness. Suddenly, a terrible voice in the dark cried, "My brothers! when Christ was fastened to the pillar by the Jews, he was *scourged!*" At these words, the bright figure disappeared, and the darkness became total. Suddenly, we heard the sound of scourges descending upon bare flesh. I cannot conceive anything more horrible. Before ten minutes had passed, the sound became *splashing,* from the blood that was flowing. . . . (*Life in Mexico,* pp. 275–276)

(All that as I longed for sleep.)

Even in Paris I am not crazy about accordion music

(perhaps a long time ago in some *bal musette* in Place Pigalle I might have liked it); and this one did seem especially horrible, his repertoire both limited and musty: "La Mer," "La Vie en Rose," even some old Trenet numbers.

The next morning Rosemary reported that even in her room, farther than mine from the scenes of festivity, the music was impossibly loud, "and so boring," she added. I agreed. We sat over coffee, both of us raw and sleepless, just as though we, too, had celebrated. And the day was somber, the sky full of rapidly moving, dark greenish-black clouds, the air heavy and menacing. We agreed that it would undoubtedly rain that afternoon, which would be a good time for taking naps—which we both much needed.

But: The festivities went on. There again at lunch a huge and costumed party, and that same goddamn amplified music, those hoary old songs, over and over, on and on. I did call down to the desk, no longer caring what I sounded like—but no one answered. I even wished that the storm, which was violent and dramatic, would knock out all the electricity, including that amplifier.

As we went out that evening, Rosemary and I, we did make a great fuss at the desk—and the gentle desk clerk on duty at that time agreed that he, too, had disliked the music.

ROSEMARY AND I had not entirely coordinated our trips, and thus she was scheduled to leave, in a van from American Express, the next day, and I the day after that, in a van supplied (for a fairly steep price) by our hotel. (Neither of us felt up to more second-class bus travel, especially not alone.)

Thus, on the day that I was more or less alone, I was still

extremely tired from all that Bastille Day noise, that horrible accordion. And the day was extremely hot. Thus, following an odd instinct, I spent the day wandering from church to church, sitting in the quiet and stony cool, and contemplating.

In the Church of the Señora de Salud, with its paintings and statues of madonnas and angels, women and children, I saw a very young Indian woman with an extremely long, thick, black braid, carrying what looked to be a brand new dark-haired baby; no husband was in attendance, and I thought of a friend of mine in San Francisco, at that time very pregnant, and wondered how it would be for each of them. (My friend, Rosie, has since had her baby, Sam, a lovely dark-haired boy, and despite a network of exceptionally kind and loving friends, her "family," she is having some problems—as is undoubtedly true of the Indian girl.) And, in the Church of Philip Neri, with its marvelous, dark, mysterious paintings (attributed to Miguel Cabrero, an eighteenth-century Mexican painter), I watched a man who stood up with both arms extended toward a statue of Christ, gesticulating, in a fury of supplication. And I thought about faith, the then-alien faith that the Spaniards brought to Mexico and imposed, some-times forcibly, on an Indian populace, along with European diseases and architectural and artistic skills. But it is surely religion that took the greatest hold on those who survived the Conquest; it is hard now to imagine a non-Catholic Mexico, and when one does, thinking of Olmecs, Zapotecs, Mayans, and Aztecs, one simply sees the same religious fervor applied to other idols, to darker and more multitudinous gods.

CONFUSION SURROUNDED the procuring of a car for my next day's trip to Mexico City (which I had thought all arranged). I learned on my return to the hotel that evening that the person summoned by the hotel was ill, or had forgotten, or something, and in this emergency the desk clerk began to call; he phoned everyone he could think of, coming up at last with a somewhat nervous-seeming middle-aged man—but a man who arrived promptly at eleven the next morning. He seemed, though, reluctant to leave the town; I noted the slowness with which he drove, his look of perplexity and his several (it seemed) deliberate wrong turns. And so at last I asked him: had he forgotten something? Was he all right?

His response was a burst of language that I could hardly understand, but I gathered at last that his wife had wanted to go to a wedding in Mexico City; she was desolate at not going to this wedding. And so I suggested the obvious: Why not bring her along, in this large and comfortable car?

In another minute we were in front of a tiny pinkish stucco house (which we actually must have been circling for quite some time), and in another minute my driver had gone in and emerged with a very pretty, very pregnant young woman—and four little girls in immaculate and painstakingly ironed party dresses, like butterflies, pastels of pink and blue and yellow. Everyone climbed in, all ready to go. (What I did not like to think about was the possibility of that family's having sat there waiting, all dressed, all perfectly turned out for Mexico City, if the unknown American woman, me, had not said, Well, come along.)

I sat in front with the husband-father-driver, the mother and small girls in the seats behind, which did not seem quite right, but I saw no way to change it. And during the almost three hours of the drive down through the hills and then across the bare dramatic plains to Mexico City, although I turned from time to time to ask some questions (silly questions, but all that I could come up with: Were they all in school? No. Had they been before to the capital? Yes), we did not really converse.

As we neared the city I began to wonder (again) about the complex issue of tipping. On the one hand, my driver and his family had had a free ride to Mexico City in a comfortable, air-conditioned car, as well as whatever share of the driver's fee he got from the hotel. On the other hand—on the other hand, I simply wanted to give him, to give them, something. And so, as we drove through the awful outlying slums, that gaudily filthy area that I now recognized as the approach to the airport, I worked out a sentence. "Here is something for some ice-cream cones for your daughters, who are so very pretty and so nice."

As I descended from the van I said my sentence and handed the father-driver a sheaf of pesos, what I had left, and we all smiled and shook hands all around, our warm, moist, foreign fingers pressing, as our smiles grew broader, and our eyes acknowledged that this was it, the end of our accidental encounter that had worked out so well for us all.

A N AFTERNOTE: As my plane, going home, flew up over some magnificent towering clouds, like a child's dream of heaven, over Baja California, I found in my seat pocket a copy of the *Mexico City News*, a new one, and looking through those sheets I came upon "Social Notes from All Over," a section that I have always enjoyed in that paper (it is almost as funny as its San Francisco counterpart). In any case, under notes from San Miguel de Allende, I read that the Señora ———— (naming the wife of the owner of our hotel), had recently celebrated the occasion of her birthday and, coincidentally, Bastille Day, with a "lively party" at her husband's hotel.

Indeed, I thought—at the same deciding that on my next trip I would be more apt to stay at the hacienda where the chair fell on my foot and where Alicia, the owner, was so very kind—with the swimming pool, and flowers. (In fact, since my own trip, two local friends have stayed *chez* Alicia; they liked it there very much—and report that she still remembers the knocked-over chair and my bright blue foot.)

CHAPTER
SIX

OAXACA

BLACK NIGHT mountains and an immense long valley full of lights, scattered, scant, and then clustered into a great and brilliant city—to which I longed, unreasonably, to go instead of to Veracruz, to which we were actually flying at that moment, R. and I, from Mexico City.

"That must be Oaxaca," R. observed.

"It looks so beautiful. Shouldn't we go there sometime?"

"You thought Detroit looked beautiful from the air, remember?"

I did not want to quarrel about my view of Detroit, nor did I want to remind R. that we were going to Veracruz because of a drunken architect whom he had met in the surf in Zihuatanejo, who had said that Veracruz was marvelous.

And I especially did not remind him of that when things in Veracruz did not work out very well (in fact, Veracruz is the only place I have ever been in Mexico to which I would not choose to go back—well, Veracruz and Tuxtla Gutiérrez). For starters, in Veracruz we were booked into an economy-class hotel, chosen from one of those five-dollars-a-day hotel guides—and it was both noisy and very ugly. And bright: A light from the stairwell shone directly, unavoidably, into our room, along with much foot-traffic noise. (This was long before

I caught onto room-changing as a standard procedure, though in that place I am not sure it would have done much good.)

Also, for once, I got sick. Not the fault of the city, but I can't help thinking: That is where I was sick.

R., out sight-seeing alone, reported back a considerable disappointment in the architecture. "If you squint your eyes it's great," he said, and described buildings that were pale and crumbling, and a very grim island fortress, San Juan of Ulua, originally built as a dungeon for dissidents and/or criminals, who drowned there as the tides came in. The fort was later used defensively against numerous invaders, most recently the United States, in 1914. R. said that it was impressive but that I would not have liked it much, he thought. "You're right, we should have jumped ship at Oaxaca," he said.

"Maybe next time."

I DID indeed very much want to go to Oaxaca; however, the very universality of enthusiasm for it somewhat put me off: D. H. Lawrence, Malcolm Lowry, even Saul Bellow, whom one does not think of as an enthusiast for scenery, have all lavished praise on lovely Oaxaca. Not to mention all the friends: "It's my favorite place, actually the prettiest in Mexico, you'll love it." One tends to resist a heavy dose of that; at least I do.

And a year or so later we did, in fact, come to Oaxaca, this time booking into what was billed as the most famous, the best hotel, an exconvent. We arrived there late at night and were shown to a room, and when we got up the next morning and opened the curtains I instantly thought, Oh, they're right, all those people, this is the prettiest place.

I saw: a small green courtyard, surrounded by old and worn streaked gray stones and edged by flower beds, profusions of bloom and color—and at one end a curious stone building that consisted of a series of overlapping stone arches, with a very large stone basin in the center. We later found that this area was called *la lavendería,* the laundry, and this is where the washing for the convent was all done—where the nuns in their habits, white ones, probably (that is how I like to imagine this), washed out their clothes, and sheets, towels, household napkins, whatever. And this is surely the most beautiful laundry, anywhere.

The next courtyard contained a small fountain, many more flowers, and more green grass, all very well tended.

The dining room consisted of open, arcaded stone halls, surrounding a great display of tropical growth—trunks and limbs and leaves and branches and flowers, everywhere brilliant flowers. And hummingbirds. And pigeons. Sitting at one of those tables, looking out into that thriving, waving mass of growth and color, seemed itself a meditation on happiness.

It seemed to us quite quintessentially Mexican, in its rich and somewhat careless magnificence—somewhat primitive, if you will. Also very Mexican seemed the fact that on that first and on most later days, some restorative painting was going on; workmen dabbed yellow spots on the massive columns supporting the arches.

From that first trip to Oaxaca, I remembered the flowers in the cloister of the convent where we stayed; the pretty *zócalo,* at that time still adrift in the detritus of Christmas; the pottery shards; the papier-mâché radishes; the dead balloons. And I remembered the somber, magnificent interiors of the churches, and the incredible spaces, the weird pyramids of Monte Albán, and the tombs of Mitla—but what I remembered most (I remember this still) from that trip was some pervasive sense of evil, of violence, a sense that one can have at any time in most places in Mexico, I know (in New York too, or in Haiti, probably, but all these intimations have their own specifics). Walking through the gorgeous church of

Santo Domingo, then, I was subject to terrifying premonitions (uncommon, for me).

And this is what happened:

The next day we were driving down the Pan-American Highway, back from Mitla (one of the two great archaeological sites, the other being Monte Albán)—where I had been further frightened, descending into dark tombs—R. and I in the back seat, our driver and a friend of his, a sort of guide-interpreter, in front. Suddenly, just ahead of us, we saw a cluster of cars, people. An ambulance. The driver's friend began to mutter to himself, and I caught some words: *Diós. Muertos. Madre.*

By the time we passed the group our car had slowed to a crawl, and we could all too easily see, stretched there on the highway, two blanket-covered bodies, one large, adult-sized; the other very small, a child. And feet: Four feet stuck out from those blankets. A woman's shabby black shoes, a child's sandals. Even the ambulance drivers, with their stretchers, seemed reluctant to approach that terrible tableau; they stood there on the highway in the sunlight, quite still. Transfixed.

And we went on, and back to our hotel.

"YOU MAKE too much of things," R. told me, at dinner. "Two people. It happens every minute. Somewhere every second. New York. Bangladesh."

"I know. But those two—the feet." I couldn't quite explain. (But that picture is still in my mind.)

SOMEONE (I believe it was Henry James) remarked that in California the historical silence is deafening—and

surely in Oaxaca the reverse must be true. Various civiliza-
tions, most of them highly complex, have inhabited that long,
rich valley for more than 11,000 years. Eleven thousand, an
impossible span of time to conceive of—and what very loud
voices must speak from all that history. Certainly one has the
sense that in Oaxaca, especially, of course, at Monte Albán,
and at Mitla. Monte Albán was built by the Zapotecs in
around 300 B.C.; by the time of the fall of Rome (A.D. 410), it
was a magnificent, thriving city. After dominating the area for
about nine hundred years, it began its mysterious decline; the
Zapotecs moved out and on, and the Mixtecs, who are
thought to have built Mitla in about the tenth century (A.D.),
continued to use it as a ceremonial area. Another theory is that
the Zapotecs built Mitla as well as Monte Albán but that they
were strongly influenced by the Mixtecs. In any case—a vast
confusion of roots, of sources.

Also, in the city of Oaxaca itself one hears or feels voices,
layers of voices. Messages. After our hotel was a convent, it
was, for a time, a prison: What a strange confusion of voices
must be embedded in those walls!

And no wonder that I was subject to dark premontions in
the Church of Santo Domingo, which was first built in the
mid-sixteenth century, shortly after the Conquest; later, during the anticlerical revolts of the eighteenth century, it was
turned into a stable and almost wrecked. Later still, and very
gradually, it was almost fully restored.

I N ANY case, I always knew that I would go back to
Oaxaca and to that hotel. And to the *lavandería*. I wanted
to have coffee in the *zócalo* and to hear some music from the
bandstand. And to see (again) the Tamayo Museum, and
Monte Albán. (Mitla drew me less, possibly because of its

association for me with that terrible highway accident, those feet.)

M Y NEXT trip began, in its planning stages, during the course of a conversation with a New York friend, an editor, Nancy, about Thanksgiving. "It's so long," we both said. "The weekend goes on and on forever. Wouldn't it be great to just skip it? Maybe we could? Maybe next year— Oaxaca?"

And so we did just that. We three, Nancy and her husband, Andrew, a doctor, and I, all met in Mexico City, and together we flew to Oaxaca, on a bright clear morning in November—over small and then larger villages, over range after range of enormous, rounded mountains, green on the lower slopes and faintly lined with small roads, or paths, and then rising, barren and wrinkled. Mountains like decaying giants.

Andrew the doctor had been sick in Mexico City (from an omelet eaten on the plane from New York, he was certain), and I thought, as we all disembarked in Oaxaca, that he still did not look well. However, the air was warm and lovely, the flowers profuse, and I thought, or hoped, that he would be better soon. (I was feeling responsible for this trip—a bad habit.)

We were herded into a large van with a number of other people, all headed for different hotels. One of the passengers with us was a very short, squat, gray-bearded German, who carried a huge camera case and a very large cigar; I very much hoped that he would not be at our hotel, but of course he was.

The hotel looked much as I remembered it, except that this time I was led in what I felt was the wrong direction, up some stairs and down halls, down passageways—to my room, very small, on the street, with no view of anything at all.

About hotel rooms: Clearly, in more ways than one, I was brought up wrong. The message that I got from those Southern small-town depression years was clearly: Take what you are given and be grateful. Which, as I have repeatedly been told in one way or another, is a considerable mistake when registering at hotels: They *expect* you to complain. And in this instance I did so, twice. The second room I was offered was just above the swimming pool and bar. But the third, final room was a beauty and just where I wanted to be—on the cloister that contained the *lavandería*.

ZÓCALO. ONE explanation for the derivation of the word is that in colonial Mexico, the period of Spanish rule, *zócalo* referred to the pedestal of a statue, and most statues, then, were of some conquering Spanish hero, a conquistador. All over Mexico, while these pedestals were waiting for their statues, appropriately placed on the main town square, the squares themselves became known as *zócalos*—as they are to this day.

The *zócalo* in Oaxaca is one of the pleasantest places that I have ever seen. It actually consists of two small plazas, one much smaller than the other and joined as a leg to the larger. Each has its own large church, its municipal building. And both squares are very busy places, scenes of much commercial and political activity, as well as of encounters of social-business-amorous natures.

As you sit at a café on the *zócalo*, at almost any hour of the day or night, over coffee or whatever, the general impression is of a rich peacefulness. Huge dark-leafed trees dominate the area; these days their trunks are painted with white lime against an infestation of ants, but far from detracting from the beauty of the trees, those white areas seem designed to harmonize with the lacy, white-painted wrought-iron benches that border the plaza. Everything there looks lacy: the leaves and the intricate wrought iron, and the fancy, elevated bandstand, with its strange bulbous-shaped dark-green tin roof, in the center of the plaza. (Where, on the other trip, we heard some mariachi music that was truly splendid, exceptional.)

On the first day of this trip, then, after so many arguments over rooms, so much coping with luggage and changes of rooms (Nancy and Andrew had also moved, though only once), a festive lunch on the *zócalo* seemed in order; having walked about a little, exclaiming at the general attractiveness of the place, we went upstairs, up over the plaza, to a restaurant overlooking the trees—a move that unhappily coincided with the start of an endless political harangue, with loudspeakers that must have carried that hysterical exhorting voice for miles, so that any conversation among the three of us was out of the question. We asked the waitress how long they would be there, and she smiled and shrugged. However, we did not actually have a great deal to say at that moment, beyond expressions of pleasure at where we were, at the *zócalo* of Oaxaca—all of which we expressed in smiles, across the beer and the excellent lunch, above the noise. (All this must have been much worse for Andrew, who had begun to feel unwell, again. Like most doctors, he is impatient with illness, especially his own.)

As we finished our lunch and came back downstairs and out onto the square, all the vendors were out in full force, with rebozos and baskets, armloads of jewelry—down to the smallest, inevitably enchanting, tiny children with their Chiclets. (I have never seen anyone buy these Chiclets, but surely someone must?) These children, these vendors of Chiclets, are

sometimes alone, or as often a dark young mother trails along
with wares of her own, some necklaces or leather bookmarks.
The mothers are young indeed, fourteen or fifteen, they look
to be. I would guess that the accompanied little children are
firstborns; with second, third, and god knows how many more
children, the mothers must, of necessity, give up on such
surveillance; those later children are the ones out selling on
their own. And what tired, sad, nearly defeated faces those
young women often have, their brief girlhoods and the moment of romance already over, years of labor and childbirth,
more labor and more childbirth almost inevitably ahead.

Still, the *zócalo* is a lovely place for a tourist to be. All
during that visit to Oaxaca I kept coming back to it, often to sit
alone over excellent coffee. I loved observing the hourly
changes on that square. That first day I came back around
dusk, and from my table I could see across the plaza and up an
open street to the distant horizon, the dark blue mountain
range that surrounds the valley of Oaxaca, against a very pale
pink sky.

I watched a tiny boy who was carrying a huge sheaf of
giant gladioli, most certainly for the altar of one of the
churches—and women who passed with large, fragrant trays
of red roses. A blind guitarist whose guide was a wiry little boy
took his stand on the terrace near where I sat; he played loudly
and enthusiastically and very badly, but fortunately not for
long. Then the little boy passed a plate around for pesos, and
they left, walking slowly along the arched stone arcades that
line the square.

MORNINGS IN Oaxaca are bright and busy. In the
courtyard dining room of our hotel, two men in painting clothes were dabbing yellow patches on the heavy

plastered columns—again, I still remembered the touching-up activity from the previous trip. Two pigeons fought furiously over a tiny scrap of bread, flailing at each other with extended wings. (This may be a form of amorous activity for pigeons that I don't know about, but I very much doubt it.) And, from the reception desk, came a long harsh sound of shouted German and the unmistakable smell of cigar smoke: The small German with the big camera and the long cigar also had a very large voice. I went out to look and there he stood, haranguing a group, most of whom seemed to listen and respond with interest.

Water from the hotel's upper floors dripped down onto the jungle of plants there in the atrium, as, up there, the floors were being watered down and swept. The flowers all looked brighter and larger and fresher than the night before, all those deep rich shades of bougainvillea and the glossy greens of philodendron leaves.

I fell into a miniconversation, somehow, with a young British engineer, who was sitting alone at breakfast with a book, as I was. He was actually an astrogeneticist, he told me, and he had come to Mexico to investigate Mayan calendars. The Mayans were far more sophisticated even than had previously been thought, he told me; they were capable of receiving messages from the sun and thus of predicting the exact moment of their own extinction.

Could this possibly be a self-fulfilling prophesy? I asked him. At a certain point they gave up and died?

He thought not, and in the book that he showed me as an illustration of his views, he pointed to a Mayan bas-relief, in which people were being murdered by the sun, screaming against its rays.

All of life is determined at the moment of conception, he told me (his eyes enlarged, neurotic-looking, too eager to please). He and his group were all concentrated on that moment, the instant of fertilization, rather than the more usual, astrological view—planetary movement at the moment of birth. (And when you think of it, one does make as much sense as the other, with his view seeming just faintly more sensible.)

When, I asked him, did he predict the demise of our own civilization?

Oh, rather clearly 1998, he said, with an apologetic smile. (If you want to be liked, it's hard to pass out bad news.)

Oh.

That seemed to be the end of our conversation, and in later encounters—in the bar, passing along a hall—we exchanged somewhat uneasy smiles: the smiles of two strangers who have had a too-serious, too-intense conversation to be able to continue with trivia. If the world is to end in eight years, what matters the state of one's health on any particular morning, even in Oaxaca?

SINCE MANY streets in Oaxaca slope gently downward toward the central plaza, the *zócalo* and its massive, tall green trees are visible from a fair distance, and thus the *zócalo,* though not on a high pinnacle, still dominates the town.

Thirty or so years ago the trees were even taller and heavier and thicker, I was told by a Mexican anthropologist who grew up in Oaxaca. When he was a child, he said, his grandfather's house was on the square, and the branches of the huge laurels reached out and touched—and darkened— the top windows of their house. It is terrible to think that this process of attrition could continue, that these trees could further diminish—like North American elms, which is what at first I thought they were.

ONCE AGAIN I saw the small boy with his blind grandfather (as I assumed he was), the guitarist; they had stopped near a bench to count up money. The little boy did the counting, of course, very businesslike, and reported the take to the old man. And I saw an American woman who sat on the curb, with the dazed and startled look of someone who has just been very sick, which, it turned out, she had. A group of Mexican workmen were busily building a broad wooden platform, presumably for another demonstration. And as I settled at my favorite café with my coffee, an Indian vendor, with long gray hair and a serape over her arm, came by and politely accepted my regrets for not buying.

Oaxaca is very much a city in which one could stay and settle in; one could live there (I think). And work there, as D. H. Lawrence did. Lawrence lived in Oaxaca during the winter of 1924–1925 (with Frieda and Lady Brett, which made for various forms of trouble); he wrote *Mornings in Mexico* about Oaxaca, and several essays. Malcolm Lowry also lived there. Oaxaca predated Cuernavaca for the Lowrys and is often referred to in *Under the Volcano.* Not to mention countless other writers and nonwriters, and painters, and plain and fancy expatriates. For me its appeal is stronger than that of San Miguel de Allende, possibly because it is a more Indian than colonial town—a fact embodied in the small and very beautiful Tamayo Museum, the first museum in Mexico in which pre-Columbian (Indian) art and artifacts were respectfully, admiringly exhibited.

It is, in fact, one of the pleasantest museums I have ever seen (reminding me, somehow, perhaps only in scale, of the lovely small museum in Verona, on the river—with its marvelous equestrian statue). The museum is housed in a former quite-small one-story townhouse, built around a pretty courtyard in which there is a beautifully carved fountain. The colors of the interior rooms were selected by Tamayo himself, and those colors arc warm and subtle, imparting a certain glow to the artifacts there. That museum, and the *zócalo*, for me epitomize the town, "Oaxaca City," as it is called by natives; both arc so gently beautiful, a life near them would be entirely possible (but then I am given to fantasies about living in various places to which I will never actually move, probably).

But the fact that the culture of Oaxaca is indigenous rather than decadent does give it more energy. The façades of the churches (there are more than twenty-five) have the look of structures put together piece by piece, rather than by any carefully worked-out design. They have an odd, rather soft, and quite irregular beauty—quite unlike the sharp edges of Gothic cathedral carving.

Santo Domingo, out near the hotel where we were staying, is certainly the most magnificent church in town, with its crisscross gold-and-white ceiling, and everywhere an overwhelming weight of gold. And if we relatively jaded tourists are quite bedazzled by such splendor, one can hardly calculate the effect on far less worldly Indians, two or three hundred years ago. It must have sent them reeling to the priests who wished to convert them, reeling blindly and agreeing to anything. In fact, it is very hard (at least for me it is hard) to look at all that gold and not to think of all the surrounding poverty, the advantage taken of relative innocence; this has always been a problem for me in Mexico—as well as in Spain, Portugal, any impoverished Catholic country.

One has to say, however, that it is still an extremely beautiful church—once you somehow come to terms with all that gold.

B Y O U R second day in Oaxaca, Andrew had recovered, but Nancy was ill, and so it was with Andrew that I went to the market, where we both wanted to buy huaraches— Andrew for gardening, I for simple comfort. This market, the Mercado Benito Juárez, is a couple of blocks from the zócalo—an enormous, unfloored building with a rounded roof of corrugated tin. And inside, among countless open stalls, one finds: everything. Chocolate, coffee, dried herring, cheeses, underwear, skirts and sweaters, shoe polish, jewelry, fruits, meats, and fish. Paintings, hardware, mirrors, furniture. Everything in the world but huaraches was what we found that first afternoon, as, dazedly, we walked past all those goods, picking our way through the crowd, over the hard uneven dirt floor. Strangely enough, in my mind there was some corner of that space to which I had been before, a corner set aside for huaraches, for lots of huaraches, that I had seen on the previous visit. However, I could sense Andrew's restiveness under a condition that must have been unfamiliar to him; a busy doctor, he probably never shops—whereas Nancy, a very New York girl, is a passionate shopper.

I now added to my lore of traveling with couples two new facts: One, when one of the couple is sick, the single person is then around for company. (Presumably, if both members of the couple were sick, that single person would be very helpful and caring, a situation that I am very glad did not arise: I would not want to take care of a sick doctor.) Two, when that sickness does occur, there is a chance for the two people who know each other least well, if that is the two healthy people, to hang out together, to become somewhat closer friends. All this is a long way of saying that I had a very good time being with Andrew, I liked him better and better; although in a general way I don't like doctors very much, I have always admired and been fond of Andrew, he has never been only a husband-of-friend.

I asked him, "What's so great about huaraches for gardening?"

"You can just hose them off when you're through, and they last forever."

"Oh."

Later that afternoon I came back to the market alone, and I headed directly, unerringly for the huaraches, as though all along there had been a map in my mind. But, curiously, I did not buy any then, partly because there were simply too many from which to choose, and I felt a vast confusion.

R OSEMARY, THE friend with whom I had gone to San Miguel, had called me before I left for Oaxaca to say that she had heard of a restaurant there to which I (we) really must go, it was said to be wonderful, she told me. El Vitral. I dutifully took down the name and almost forgot it until, as we arrived at the Oaxaca airport, a small boy was handing out advertising cards—for El Vitral. I foolishly did not grasp the sinister implications of this coincidence, but instead, one night I had our concierge call and reserve. Three for dinner, at 8:30.

After one margarita in our own hotel bar, we set out along the darkened streets for the given address, which we reached with no trouble at all. There was a jazzy green sign, announcing El Vitral. As we opened the door, though, we were greeted by a man who seemed more than a little crazy, or drugged; he stared and grinned at us so hard, so fixedly, as he gestured that we were to go upstairs to the dining room, that we were a little scared.

Upstairs the decor was all pink—pink walls and pink-shaded lamps (reminding me strongly of a restaurant in Barcelona, called Amor Lur). The effect here was far less elegant but similarly anachronistic. This place looked quite whorish, though, very louche. At one table sat a large group of very polite, smiling, and proper-looking Chinese tourists (no doubt drawn in by the same shady practice that had got to us—airport advertising). Otherwise there was no one, certainly no Mexicans. From somewhere a tape played a stirring rendition of "Fascination," and then "Jealousy." And those two queer rhythms alternated the whole time that we were there, which, in retrospect, seems very long indeed—lots of "Fascination," lots of "Jealousy."

After a very ordinary but quite prolonged meal, during which the Chinese table paid and left, as we waited for our check, a whole new group came in. A very odd group indeed, they looked like thirties' gangsters: fat men, Mexican style, with wide mustaches and big cigars and shiny slick black hair. And girls: girls with stiletto heels and black net stockings, miniskirts and large red flowers nestled in glossy black curls. Terrific eye makeup, the heaviest possible black mascara and liner, the darkest blue shadow. They looked like hatcheck girls in a movie about Prohibition. It was funny, really, but we certainly did not laugh, as we tried not to stare. I think we were even a little frightened, and certainly we wondered why we had come to this spooky place.

Just as we were about to leave, at last, the lunatic greeter came up to our table, seemingly much crazier than before. He began then to shout questions at us: Had we enjoyed our dinner? Had we really enjoyed it? Was the service really satisfactory?

It was very scary, and from the look of things he was the owner. Waiters scattered from his path with deferential scurryings.

Fortunately for us, he quite soon turned away to the far

more glamorous table to our right and became engrossed in a conversation there, forgetting us entirely, so that we were able to pay up and escape.

Back out on the streets, we felt that the whole town now had a sinister look, and we walked very fast, talking very quietly among ourselves, all the mercifully short distance to our hotel.

So much for secondhand recommendations.

"NO, THERE is very little drug use in Oaxaca. People can't afford it, you know? Even the retired people here are not generally rich, not like in Cuernavaca or Guadalajara. A nice type of people they are here, and their children who come to see them do not use drugs. I could bet on that."

These hopeful sentiments were uttered by a woman named Dorothy González, a North American married to a Mexican, who had lived in Oaxaca since 1951, when she came down from Chicago as a touring student. She now headed the small but very good American library of Oaxaca, whence we had been directed by friends.

Dorothy: a pleasantly efficient-looking woman of more or less indeterminate age. She was eager to show us around the library and to recommend books on Oaxaca and on Mexico in general (I noticed, though, that her recommendations were all a little dated: Anita Brenner, Rosa King, Ross Parmenter) and to express a certain disapproval of factual inaccuracies in other writers, notably D. H. Lawrence. She was not, however, especially forthcoming about her own life, which I found of enormous imaginative interest.

Picture, as I tried to, a young woman (I would put her in her late twenties, in 1951) coming to Mexico on a tour. And meeting a Mexican guide, a handsome one, of course. Falling in love with him and entering into a connection that would almost have had to be clandestine, at first. And, unfamiliar with Latin culture, very likely with Latin men, and being a woman of considerable intelligence, how she must have wondered what was going on: Is he always like this? Does he say all these things to every virginal American girl student?

It is quite a wonderful story, and one that Dorothy González shyly, neatly, and entirely evades the telling of, only saying that her husband speaks five languages, that one of her sons is also a guide, and that it is wonderful that all her children and grandchildren live so near that she sees them all the time.

Also in the library we met a young Canadian woman who was writing a book on women in Mexico, mostly working women; maids, factory workers, et cetera. She told us that her professor in Connecticut, a Mexican-American whom she described as a liberated man, told her that *machismo* no longer exists in Mexico. Whereas a group of young women in Oaxaca had recently (more or less in chorus) said to her, "In Oaxaca there are no men, only *machos.*" All of which had a sad and rather familiar ring.

EARLY ON in this visit to Oaxaca, in the lobby of our hotel I met some San Francisco people whom I rather slightly know (I had seen them mostly in Zihuatanejo, actually), and they said that they had hired a driver, a great one, in Oaxaca. David Sánchez. They gave me his card. They were waiting for him at that very moment, in fact, and would tell him that I might call.

That night I was summoned from dinner at the hotel to the telephone—so odd: Hardly anyone knew precisely where I was. It was David Sánchez, who very pleasantly wanted to assure me that he was available and would be most happy to drive me and my friends. Perhaps to Monte Albán? This seemed a little pushy; unimaginatively, I did not at first consider local desperation for work. On the other hand he was intelligent—and nice-sounding. And so, having already decided that we wanted to go to Monte Albán, we called David Sánchez the next morning.

He arrived very promptly at 9:30 on the specified day. (I had thought, correctly, that later in the day would be very hot on that broad, high platform which is Monte Albán, uplifted to the sun.)

David: an "Indian" face (God knows from what tribe, or tribal mix), though not as dark as his hero, Benito Juárez (the nineteenth-century political leader, governor of Oaxaca, then president of Mexico, and the author of much liberal reform— a pure-blooded Zapotec Indian, from Oaxaca). A wide friendly mouth, some steel teeth, a large nose, and very dark eyes, far apart.

Andrew sat up in front with David, Nancy and I in back, and we headed out of town. David was an immediately informative talker, pointing out churches, markets, and a new neighborhood of houses for workers in which, he said, unhappily nothing worked—although they looked so nice, small stucco cottages with wonderful views of the surrounding hills.

We told David how very much we liked Oaxaca, how very pretty we thought it was. We all liked the low-lying, low-key quality of the architecture. That was because of earthquakes, David told us, and he asked me about the most recent San Francisco earthquake (that October eighty-nine quake took place about a month before this visit to Oaxaca).

I told him that I had been in Toronto, in fact on my way home at the time of the actual quake, but that I was at home for a lot of the aftershocks. And, as I had not mentioned to Andrew and Nancy, here in Oaxaca I had been feeling a lot more aftershocks—imaginary ones, I thought, reliving the trauma.

But: "Here in Oaxaca we have small earthquakes all the time," David informed us. "We worry if for several days we have no earthquake. That way we don't get big ones, like you had."

There was, in this, a faintly smug implication that Oaxaca dealt with the problem of earthquakes much more efficiently than San Francisco did, and geologically speaking one could agree—although there have been, in Oaxaca, several major and devastating earthquakes, most notably in twenty-eight and thirty-one, both well before the birth of David Sánchez.

From the road leading up to Monte Albán one gets a sweeping view of the whole valley of Oaxaca, rich and green and dotted here and there with settlements, clusters of dwellings, farms—and church towers. And, there is Oaxaca City itself; you can make out the dark massed trees of the *zócalo* and the tower of Santo Domingo.

We arrived at a large parking area and walked up and through a very unprepossessing museum—and out to the incredible space that is Monte Albán. Not "use of space," in the current sense, but space itself, offered up to the sky, to whatever lurking gods might be around. Even when you are standing there, looking down at the very broad, flat field, with pyramids on either side and one in the middle, you know that you are looking at a larger area than you can imaginatively grasp.

We walked all around the edge, beside the steep, flat-topped pyramids, with their high, very narrow stairs, which we all decided not to climb. And we walked out among some trees and bushes to a sort of lookout point, to see again that wide green view of the valley.

From everywhere that day there wafted a smell of wild cilantro. And of hot dust, and dried dung.

Strict national laws prevent the exportation of genuine artifacts, pre-Columbian, from Mexico—laws that came much too late, after scandalous wholesale plundering of tombs; still, in the bushes surrounding Monte Albán there lurk rather scruffy-looking hawkers, with shards of pottery extended toward the gringos (or Germans, or Mexican tourists, probably), along with loud whispered assurances that these are genuine, true artifacts from the ruins here at Monte Albán. Or from the tombs at Mitla.

We stayed there for quite a while, standing about and marveling, trying and failing to stretch our imaginations back to that ancient civilization, quite possibly three thousand years back, this piece of land that had been occupied by at least three groups, or tribes.

Each of these groups contributed many skillful and some inspired artisans of gold and ceramic objects, most of which were carted off, in one way or another. I myself remember as a child, sometime during the thirties, hearing about newspaper reports of fabulous discoveries of buried gold in Mexico.

Also, in theory, there are around ninety-two thousand ruins in and around Oaxaca that still remain unexplored.

WHILE WE were walking around Monte Albán, David, in the car, in the increasing heat, had occupied himself with sketching; he showed us a sketchbook full of faces. The last one was of Andrew, which David presented to Andrew and Nancy (very wise of him, I thought, to have done Andrew rather than Nancy or me; I'm afraid women tend to have less sense of humor about their faces than men do).

David took us next to what he told us was the oldest

church in Oaxaca, a white, rather small structure standing a little forlornly up and back from the road, in a large bare yard. With, inside, incredible displays of gold. And flowers, masses of white gladioli everywhere (according to Andrew, what in New York would be thousands of dollars worth of flowers).

L ATER, DAVID showed us some slightly sentimental but nice studies of little girls—his own, he told us. David, at twenty-seven, had five children—and he told us in somewhat surprising detail about how birth control did not work; although he and his wife went dutifully to the clinic and "did everything" they were told to do, still five children arrived. (One wonders, a little, about the nature of instruction.) David smiled as he said all this, he was obviously a man who loved his wife and daughters. But still . . .

We asked David about political parties in Mexico, pretending (easily enough) even greater ignorance than we in fact possessed. Both the traditional PRI and the newer PAN are entirely parties of the rich, David said, and both hopelessly corrupt. We asked then about the Cardenistas, the new party under the leadership of Cuauhtemoc Cárdenas. David's voice and his eyes warmed and lightened as he told us that Cárdenas was the greatest man in Mexico since Juárez—and that in fact it was he who won the last election, not Salinas. (I had recently read an article in a San Francisco paper describing Cárdenas as the only possibly hope for Mexico—an honest and intelligent man, a possibly great politician. And so I was curious about him.)

David told us that at one time he had been a political cartoonist for the local paper. And the mayor had become so enraged with his cartoons that he made threats against

David's life, David said—although he did not make it entirely clear why this was so.

AFTER THE oldest church, David took us to Teo-titlán, a town inhabited by Zapotec weavers—the best of whom, David said, was a friend of his named Isaac.

We left the main highway for a narrow road leading up into the hills and then arrived at the village. Our approach, as usual in small Mexican towns, was marked by sleepy dogs who slowly rose from their center-of-street siestas and ambled off with a bored and reproachful look at the intruding car—and by a cluster of tiny girls in school uniforms, led along by a small, dark, smiling nun. We turned off the main street, onto an even less populous road—and arrived at Isaac's.

First there was the weaving room. Four very wide looms were all in action; the weavers, three men and a very merry-looking young woman, were all at work there. In fact, all four of those people, their quite incredibly nimble fingers working—literally flying—back and forth, looked amazingly happy, I thought. They did not look in the least impatient with what must at times have been dull drudgery. Up on the walls behind them were some designs for more rugs—and all around hung long skeins of wool, in marvelous dark rich colors.

Across a courtyard, passing stray chickens and a few round, wide-eyed children, we met Isaac and some of his family. Isaac, a small, gray-haired, intensely energetic and pleasantly voluble man, seemed surrounded by busy, helpful women of various ages. Together they showed us how the wool was carded, then spun on the spinning wheel—as Isaac explained that they also made all their own dyes. From a cactus plant that conveniently stood just next to him, he picked up a tiny insect, which he then crushed with his thumbnail—so that a rich dark stain appeared: cochineal.

The hall of rugs was indeed impressive, some enormous rugs for baronial halls, along with small scatter rugs, in a vast variety of bold designs. (A few years ago a San Francisco friend who was remodeling his house on Potrero Hill went down to this very place to have a rug made for his winding central staircase—a great long serpent which is red, cochineal.) Nancy and Andrew bought a small Indian-abstract for their house in Sag Harbor.

W E PARTED from David at the Hotel Victoria, which is up out of town, on a hill.

And it was only as we sat at lunch in the nice glass-walled dining room, with its splendid valley view, that any of us remembered that today was actually Thanksgiving.

CHAPTER
SEVEN

CUERNAVACA

TWO MOUNTAIN *chains traverse the republic roughly from north to south, forming between them a number of valleys and plateaus. Overlooking one of these valleys, which is dominated by two volcanoes, lies, six thousand feet above sea level, the town of Quauhnahuac. It is situated well south of the Tropic of Cancer, to be exact on the nineteenth parallel, in about the same latitude as the Revillagigedo Islands to the west in the Pacific, or, very much further west, the southernmost tip of Hawaii—and as the port of Tzucox to the east on the Atlantic seaboard of Yucatan near the border of British Honduras, or, very much further east, the town of Juggernaut, in India, on the Bay of Bengal.*

The walls of the town, which is built on a hill, are high, the streets and lanes tortuous and broken, the roads winding. A fine American-style highway leads in from the north but is lost in its narrow streets and comes out a goat track. Quauhnahuac possesses eighteen churches and fifty-seven cantinas. It also boasts a golf course and no less than four swimming pools, public and private, filled with water that ceaselessly pours down from the mountains, and many splendid hotels.

These two paragraphs, which open Malcolm Lowry's magnificent *Under the Volcano*, describe Cuernavaca sometime in the late thirties, and while I did not believe that present-day Cuernavaca could bear much resemblance to the Quauhnahuac of the novel, nor to the actual Cuernavaca of Lowry's time there, still I suppose I had in mind some possible trace, some permanent geographic fact common to all of "Cuernavaca." Or, perhaps, some lingering emanations: I hoped for ghosts.

Also, more practically, from the safe distance of San Francisco, Cuernavaca seemed a safe and reasonable choice for a week or so alone, after my Thanksgiving in Oaxaca with Nancy and Andrew. And it would be not only the lack of Nancy and Andrew that I would feel; Cuernavaca would also represent my first venture without R.

And in fact, about twenty years back I had once spent a couple of nights in Cuernavaca with R., and I remembered from that time an interestingly reconstructed cathedral and a very pretty motel, with broad terraces down to a good swimming pool—and a memorable dinner at Las Mañanitas: Sputnik appeared in the sky above us, as we ate and drank on the outdoor terrace, among peacock and flowers. I had wanted to go back there, though not especially alone.

In Mexico City, before going to Oaxaca, I had arranged to meet a driver with his car there, at the hotel in Mexico City. In a rather battered Oldsmobile, Ernesto Solario and I drove out through the endless sprawl of the outskirts of Mexico City, out through San Angel and Coyoacán, past Pedregal and the university, until (it seemed quite sudden) we were out in the true countryside, on a well-maintained highway, that (strangely) reminded me very much of the beautiful parkways in Westchester County in the thirties, the Sawmill River Parkway, the Bronx River Parkway. Part of the reminder may have come from somewhat similar contrasts: the grimy poverty of Mexico City and this lush and spacious landscape. Rural North Carolina, the modest college town where I came from, and lavish Westchester, where I used to visit relatives who were rich (and conservative: the depression did not exist, they thought).

And there before us, quite suddenly, as large and unreal as clouds, were Malcolm Lowry's two volcanos, Popocatépetl and, far less distinct, Ixtacihuatl, the former larger and clearer, more white—the latter distant, pale blue. I had not thought of a possibly beautiful drive, and this seemed a present, a lovely surprise.

We were passing, then, some prosperous-looking farms, broad sweeps of grassy fields with here and there an acre of wheat sheaves, all tidily bound up like little wigwams, and now golden in the slowly waning sunlight. I began to feel foolishly optimistic about Cuernavaca; I see now that sometimes reading what you take to be natural signs can be a serious error, and that golden wheat sheaves did not necessarily mean that I would be okay in Cuernavaca—alone.

About midway, though, we went through a very small, very poor-looking town, called Tres Marias; it seemed a reminder of the reality of Mexico, extreme poverty rather than golden wheat sheaves and blue-shadowed snowy peaks.

R EACHING THE outskirts of Cuernavaca, Ernesto was uncertain as to the address of my hotel, and to his credit he stopped and asked (interesting, in terms of *machismo;* I am thinking of the frequent comment made by American women, myself among them, that men will never stop to ask directions). And, as we drove where we had been told to, Ernesto asked me how I was getting back to Mexico

City. Would I need a driver? I hedged, only saying that it was possible that I might, and I took his phone number.

At the hacienda, where I had paid for a room for a week, I was shown to a very small room near the entrance, very clean and bare, and very noisy, as things turned out. But in some flagging of energy, or nerve, I took it anyway and more or less settled in.

The grounds, though, of this former hacienda of a Spanish count, and present weekend resort, were quite grand: acres of painstakingly tended green lawns, with a small pond of fat, lethargic goldfish and a small bridge across the pond, I guess for goldfish viewing. Impressive trees, tall and thickly leafed out, of substantial girth; and luxuriant vegetation: philodendron, spathoflorae. And a two-story guesthouse, all hung with flowering bougainvillea, in its usual panoply of pinks and red and mauves. Curiously, these grounds, too, reminded me of Westchester, of luxury among the rich and rare in the far-off thirties.

In any case, this would be a good place to be alone, I thought, or at least it would be perfectly okay, and I went into the dining room as early as possible. Alone. I had walked through the bar on the way in, a very strange, very retro "hunting room," dominated by the immense head of a very black bull and otherwise decorated with several rows of snakeskins and the pelt of a tiny leopard—but I think it was the menacing bull's head that made me decide not to have a drink there after all.

I was alone in the dining room, except for two white-haired, rather pious-looking ladies, perhaps teachers of some sort, librarians, who came in and sat some distance from my table. And then a pleasant-looking couple came in, a man and a woman, who seemed attractively fond of each other, but who then seemed to set about drinking a really inordinate amount. Having little to distract me, I counted their intake:

three margaritas apiece, two bottles of wine. But they continued to look cheerful and healthy—as I began to dislike the fact
of having dinner alone and generally to dislike the fact of
traveling alone, to Cuernavaca.

This feeling, this isolation, was confirmed the next day,
as I swam and read, or rather tried to read, beside the pool.
More happy couples abounded, including an extremely handsome and amorous pair, young Mexicans, clearly on their
honeymoon, or their first trip away as lovers. Most of the other
guests were, in fact, Mexican, middle-class Mexicans (which
is to say rich) off on long weekend vacations, the only Americans beside myself being the two schoolteacher types and the
nice-looking couple who drank so much.

And the woman of that couple appeared beside the pool
soon after I had arrived, and we fell into a desultory conversation—or not so very desultory: We exchanged lives, as travelers will (though actually it was she who talked, and I gave
almost nothing in exchange, certainly not what I did for a living). Her name was Martha, and her husband's name (as I had
somehow thought, this was a second marriage) was Harry,
and, curiously, they had been married to people named Harry
and Martha before, respectively. They had between them
seven children, all doing well. In fact, the children were doing
so well, financially, that Martha and Harry, this Martha and
Harry, had decided to leave the "bulk of their estate" to a
washroom in a national park on the Olympic Peninsula, to put
in more showers. I wondered what sort of plaque would be
put up in their honor—THE MARTHA AND HARRY _____ ME-
MORIAL SHOWERS?—but I felt that I could not ask. Martha
suggested that we go together to Las Mañanitas, the locally
famous and very beautiful restaurant where I had been before
with R. I agreed; I wanted to see it again.

At the desk, along with making a reservation for the next
day's lunch at Las Mañanitas, I arranged for a change of room

119

(a better room would cost sixty dollars, I found, as opposed to the forty I was paying for my cell); and I mentioned my need for a car and a driver to Mexico City. Also, I announced my plan for that day, which was to walk to the center of town, the *zócalo*.

This last was greeted with expressions of doubt, if not downright disapproval; too far, not a pleasant walk, and, again, too far. All of which only served to make me persist in my plan.

Most annoyingly, they turned out to be right, that chorus of naysayers at the desk: It was not at all a pleasant walk, it was indeed too far and too hot, and furthermore, those streets were overwhelmed with traffic fumes. I walked along a winding, not-wide avenue, on a narrow sidewalk, past great walled villas with quantities of pointed shards of glass embedded in the tops of the walls. You could just glimpse the houses through the heavy iron gates.

I was thinking about Malcolm Lowry and Margerie Bonner, his wife, and about the Consul and Yvonne and Hugh and their beautiful, mysterious, and accursed Cuernavaca—and I wondered where I was.

In many of these villas, retired Americans announced their presences with fairly ornate brass plaques: *Col. E. B. Johnson, USMC, Ret.,* or *Mr. and Mrs. Luther Webster,* or just, *The Harmons.* And the villas alternated with small stucco houses with large glass windows, many of which housed doctors. The Mexican custom of advertising medical specialties with large signs makes for quite alarming roadside reading; even the most established and respectable specialties— cardiology, urology—look quite wild and scary when translated into that colorful, gaudy language and written out in an ornately flourishing script. I saw *Señora Rosa Hernandez, Psiquiatría;* whoever would go to a *psiquiatría?*

As I approached the *zócalo* the street narrowed and

converged with smaller streets, a tangle of thoroughfares that rose and fell away in curious small hills, as sidewalks suddenly broke off, to reappear a few blocks later, unimproved, still broken and uneven.

The center, when you come to it, is hard to recognize as such, at first. There are actually three small adjoining squares, but the cathedral is several blocks away. (Cuernavaca is one of the few cities in Mexico whose cathedral is not actually on the zócalo.) That first morning, a Sunday, the squares were filled with long stalls selling silver jewelry, pounds and pounds of totally uninteresting earrings, necklaces, et cetera. I was looking for a birthday present for a young friend, Kate, age ten; her mother has just allowed Kate to have her ears pierced—but everything looked so much alike that I could find nothing. And in that setting even a wonderful pair of earrings would have looked much like the others—would have looked boring, mass-produced.

I walked through the streets that fanned out from those squares, past small shops as alike and as undistinguished in their way as was the jewelry. There were cheap imitations of "folk art," awful carved birds and heads of "Indians," some terrible painted leather, and the ubiquitous big black velvet sombreros. Mass-manufactured versions of formerly handmade lace and leather goods. I was quite struck by one narrow, red-tiled store, called Stress (in large jagged letters, like streaks of lightning), a boutique advertising casual clothes for ladies and gentlemen—but the clothes inside were, again, poor imitations of cheap American clothes.

With considerable relief I left all that and headed up toward the cathedral, and the Borda Gardens.

There was an enormous crowd outside the cathedral, several tour buses and their Sunday-excited occupants, all bouncing about with cameras and guidebooks. In part to avoid all that, at least for a while, I went up into the Borda

Gardens, and there, in the small entrance area, were several little white signs:

Le Gusta este jardín
  que es suyo?
Evite que sus hijos
  Lo destroyan.

and the initials, "M. L."

This is, of course, the sign that appears and reappears in Lowry's novel.

> The Consul stared at the words on the sign without moving. You like this garden? Why is it yours? We evict those who destroy! Simple words, simple and very terrible words, words which took one to the very bottom of one's being, words which, perhaps a final judgment on one, were nevertheless unproductive of any emotion whatsoever, unless a kind of colorless cold, a white agony, an agony chill as that iced mescal drunk in the Hotel Canada on the morning of Yvonne's departure. (*Under the Volcano,* 128)

Those signs were fairly white and new-looking, and so I asked the uniformed man at the inner desk about their origin.

No, they were not new signs, he told me. The signs had always been there.

And the signature? I asked. The initials, M. L.?

The initials had always been there too, I was informed. They were a part of the sign, and he had no idea as to their significance.

Trying a more direct tack, I asked if he had heard of a writer, English, who had at one time lived here in Cuernavaca and passed many afternoons in these gardens, which he had mentioned in a book.

No, he was quite unfamiliar with that name; after all, so many writers came to Cuernavaca; many of them were associated with the local language school: Perhaps I should inquire at the school for that particular writer? I might easily find him there.

I said I thought not, and he repeated that many, many American writers come to Cuernavaca, and surely most of them would find these gardens pleasant and agreeable?

Not finding the gardens especially agreeable myself, just unimaginatively laid-out gardens, not well kept up, and deeply puzzled as to the date and origin of the cryptic signature, I left for the cathedral.

This cathedral was founded in 1529, by Cortés, and was originally intended as a Franciscan monastary. Reconstructed many times in the intervening decades and centuries, it retains much of its original, somewhat stark and forbidding character. In its most recent incarnation, a bare "contemporary" look has been achieved, partly by way of some nonrepresentational stained-glass windows. On the Sunday morning that I was there a mariachi mass was in progress, which no doubt explained the tour buses and crowds. And the music was indeed quite wonderful—almost the best mariachi music I had ever heard, delivered by an elegantly costumed band, whose members wore enormous ecclesiastic smiles. On Sunday morning.

Leaving that square, after first visiting a much smaller and prettier church beside the cathedral, a church with a marvelously irregular carved stone façade and a lovely belfry, I started back to the *zócalo*. And was temporarily diverted by a nice huarache store, where I bought two pair, one brown and one bright yellow, which I have been wearing ever since.

The Cortés palace, on the *zócalo,* must be one of the grimmest (in fact, one of the very few grim) structures in Mexico. It is squarish, of dark-gray stone, the effect not softened by a double tier of arches in the center of its façade. It looks like what it is, or was: a fortress. One sees it as Cortés's own fortress against the Mexican people, and it suggests that he had at least some idea how deeply he had wronged the indigenous population. These days it is, naturally, a museum, housing displays of warlike artifacts—and some huge and most impressive Rivera murals, depicting the history of Mexico, with emphasis on its bloodier, most exploitative aspects.

THE NEXT day's lunch with Martha at Las Mañanitas was mildly pleasant. The place itself looked far less glamorous than I remembered it, the difference, of course, being that between noon and night, not to mention the twenty-year gap in time. It looked just slightly shabby on this occasion, the peacock's tails less proud, more dragging on the still-precise lawns, and their cries were less raucous, their strut less certain of direction.

Our lunch itself was unmemorably good—in fact, it is hard for me to recall any meals of real excellence in Mexico, except for the stray marvel of fresh shrimp, or *huachinango*, or the really first-rate guacamole, redolent of cilantro. That day at Las Mañanitas we had, I think, very good French onion soup and some nice fresh garlicky shrimp, also good.

And Martha had two margaritas and talked quite a lot (I virtuously stuck to iced tea and listened). Harry worked for an oil company (this is interesting: No one who works for an oil company ever names the company); they lived in Houston and periodically made these sorties into Mexico to inspect the oil equipment. Which used to be fun, but now Martha really hated it. They went mostly to these really grungy places— comparatively speaking, Cuernavaca was a total treat. They never knew anyone. I asked if they met with Mexican oil people, men doing more or less the same sort of work. No, never. Martha had never met a Mexican oilman, nor the wife of any such. She spoke a little Spanish, Harry none. Harry thought the whole Mexican economy was going down the tubes, any minute. Fast. "And guess who isn't going to bail them out," she laughed.

After coffee we walked all the way back to our hotel, a distance of some three or four miles, through streets that have in retrospect become indistinguishable to me from others in the outlying districts of various Mexican cities: Cuernavaca, Guadalajara, Mérida, Tuxtla Gutiérrez—and Mexico City itself, the vastest and dirtiest, most teeming and sprawling of all Mexican cities, the horrifying prototype. We passed awful stores and tawdry hotels and movie theaters (none, though, was playing *Las Manas de Orloff,* with Peter Lorre, as in *Volcano*); we were sprayed with noxious fumes from bulging and quite decrepit school buses, from which emerged an array of brown-eyed children, mostly thin and solemn, and staring. Past improbable doctors' notices and high-walled acres of gardens, their mansions housing either very rich Mexicans or plain, retired, somewhat upper-middle-class Americans.

BACK AT the desk of our hotel, I was told that Ramón Sánchez would be my driver to Mexico City the following day, and also that a Tomás Rivera had called me, leaving a number. The name meant nothing, and almost no one knew where I was, and so mostly out of curiosity I dialed the number from my room and got Sr. Tomás Rivera, who announced that he would be my driver to Mexico City.

That was very kind, I said, but the hotel had already arranged for a driver. Another driver.

Might he ask the name of that driver?

I hesitated, but saw no reason (or no reasonable excuse) not to tell him. Ramón Sánchez.

Oh, well. Ramón was a good friend. With him it was all arranged. Ramón was actually unavailable on that day, and so it was he, Tomás Rivera, who was to be my driver.

He was quite convincing; still, not liking the possibility that Ramón Sánchez had simply been jettisoned for the convenience or the profit of Tomás Rivera, I took this whole problem out to the front desk and found another shift of people there—who assured me that it was all perfectly in order. Tomás Rivera was a most excellent driver, it would be of no importance to Ramón Sánchez.

That night I had a phone call from Ernesto Solario, who had originally driven me down from Mexico City. He wondered if possibly I needed a driver for my return. Assuring him that I was well taken care of in that way, as I hung up I felt both guilty and sorry—all these later negotiations had made me uneasy.

FROM MY new, large, high-up room I had a superior view of all the grounds, the brilliant, hourly tended flower beds, the small fountain that splashed into the pool of sleepy fat goldfish, the bougainvillea-covered cottage across the way. And the green, the endless perfect velvet of those endlessly rolling lawns, where the perfectly plumed white peacock strolled and occasionally bent to inspect a pebble in the sinuous, perfectly laid-out garden path.

I had succeeded, I felt, in finding no connection whatsoever between Malcolm Lowry's Cuernavaca and the one that I myself came upon, somewhat reluctantly, in the fall of 1989 (in November, actually, the month of the Day of the

Dead). And what I had mostly learned was what I already knew, which is that traveling alone to resorts is probably, on the whole, not a great idea.

THE NEXT day at breakfast the room was suddenly full of decorations for Christmas. Miniature Christmas trees bloomed on each table, and awful tinsel looped down from the ceiling, down over the wrought-iron chandeliers and across all the terrible paintings of sunsets and Indians. There was even, on the central table, a small Santa Claus—appallingly incongruous. In fact, in these tropical gardens, this April weather, the whole idea of Christmas seemed incongruous, impossibly distant.

AT THE appointed time I was told that my driver was there, and I went out to find not one but two men and a very small car. I somehow imagined that the two would be Ramón Sánchez and Tomás Rivera but was told that this was Tomás Rivera and his "cousin" and that the cousin would be driving me to Mexico City. Feeling that I had been somehow duped, or used, I also felt that there was nothing I could do about it at this late moment, and so I set off with the cousin, whose name was Jesús, and the drive again was very beautiful, Popocatépetl now golden in the midday sunlight. Cuernavaca farther and farther behind us and, ahead, Mexico City, and for me the plane to San Francisco.

CHAPTER
EIGHT

MÉRIDA
AND
THE YUCATÁN

HE TIME LAG between the planning of and arranging for a trip and its actuality, your departure, is surely far too long, in these overcrowded days of required far-in-advance reservations for almost anywhere. You will have in some way changed in the interval since you first thought of those particular places, those hotels, that airline schedule; and now, in the shortening days before you leave, this whole trip seems much less a good idea than it once did: You have an unexpected increase in work that you would like to do; you also have a new friend whom you will both miss and find it hard to write to, since you don't know him very well and besides, mail deliveries will be uncertain from your destination; and your cats all look to be too old to be left for long; and the bulbs that you planted in pots just outside the door, on the deck, are just about to bloom, and on your trip you will miss them entirely.

Several of these conditions prevailed as I planned and then took a trip to Mérida and Palenque—and, for a person who has always believed herself to be a very good trip planner, I managed considerable confusion. By way of excuse I might add that several other people with their divergent needs were involved; still, it was I who made the arrangements, finally.

The two other people who were to meet me more or less

en route were Janet, a writer and an old friend from New York—and Cynthia, a more recent friend, a painter who lives just outside Chicago and who often visits and shows her work in San Francisco, which is where we had met and talked about this trip. These two women had never met, and while I knew or believed them both to be kind and considerate, as well as highly talented, successful in their fields, in a hostess way (Southern women are lifelong hostesses, no matter what else is going on) I worried about their getting along, enjoying the trip and each other, and me. Also, we all had varying work requirements: I wanted to see and to write about as much of the Yucatán as possible (I had not been there before); Janet wanted to visit the local craft shops and to buy some things (she had a magazine commission); and Cynthia, a water-colorist, requires bright sunlight and interesting flowers or trees—she had also been in the Yucatán before and wished, reasonably enough, to see some new places.

We settled, then, on Mérida, where I would meet Janet; I had heard conflicting versions of that city from friends and from books, but I tended to think that it would be interesting and certainly worth seeing. Then we would go to Campeche; Campeche worked out in terms of Cynthia's schedule from Chicago, and on the map it looked like a nice beach resort, which is how a couple of guidebooks described it—a small "undiscovered" resort.

Then we would go to Palenque. We all looked forward to Palenque, the famous Mayan ruins rising from the midst of the jungles of Chiapas, in the Yucatán—not far from the Guatemalan border. (I think the Mexican discoveries, tombs full of gold, that I heard of as a child must have been in Palenque.) Then San Cristóbal de las Casas, in Chiapas, which was supposed to contain marvels of baroque architecture and to be surrounded by wildly beautiful scenery. From San Cristóbal we would go back by way of Mérida and then by various routes back to our respective homes.

THE TRIP began for me with an odd vignette in the San Francisco airport, to which I had been taken by the new friend, D., a doctor from Vermont. Ahead of us in the check-in line was a young couple, all dressed for rough travel, with backpacks, and three or four huge boxes, at least four feet square, which they were laboriously checking through, while we and everyone else impatiently waited.

An early point of contention with D. had arisen from our quite divergent attitudes toward what used to be called "the young," by which we both meant the sixties' generation, the age of both our children. To summarize, he was very antisixties, I very pro. Thus, D. saw this couple as clear proof of his case: "—so inconsiderate. Have they thought of having those boxes smelled by some dogs?" (This last was a joke, but of course with some serious intent.)

We now skip to my arrival at my designated seat on the plane, where I found that the two people next to me, on the window and middle seats, were (of course) the young couple of the enormous boxes, with whom I fell into conversation. And (this was quite incredible, I thought at the time, and in fact still think) those two were *both doctors*, and, more incredible yet, *both from Vermont*. They spoke in the same accents that I found attractive in D., and their huge boxes contained not dope but equipment for a project on infantile diarrhea in Chiapas; they were going to San Cristóbal, as was I. And they were very nice indeed, wry, very knowledgeable about Mexico in general and especially about Chiapas. It would be extremely cold there, they said, among other bits of information—a warning to which I did not pay much heed, rather thinking that it came too late, which it did.

Mostly, I could not wait to write to D. about all this. I would do so, I decided, in the Mexico City airport, where I had a fairly long wait before the plane to Mérida.

The next odd (and perhaps ominous) event took place in the airport in Puerto Vallarta, where everyone had to disembark and show tourist cards and where I was inexplicably not given a reboarding pass. I explained this omission to various officials, in the midst of the milling crowds, and received no useful answers.

And this is a basic problem, in fact, with Mexican travel, generally: Minor discomforts and anxieties, so often viewed as major by middle-class, middle-aged North Americans (of which I am certainly one), are not taken with great seriousness by Mexicans, official or otherwise. In this case I failed to impress anyone with the seriousness of my plight, although I kept trying, going about from one uniform to another—until I saw that the flight I had been on was indeed reboarding. Frightened, I watched the young doctors from Vermont out there with the others, and then, only then, was I able to persuade the official at the gate to let me back on, without a pass.

ARRIVED, FINALLY, in Mexico City, I sat down eagerly to write my letter. I had providently brought along paper and U.S.-stamped envelopes, my plan being to find some returning travelers along the way who would mail my letters to D. from whatever destinations were theirs, in the States. Thus, after finishing this letter, which was long, all that about the doctors from Vermont and my trauma in Vallarta— I began to walk about the terminal (this was not easy, I was more than a little impeded by heavy carry-on bags) in search of a returning-to-the-States American. Which was not as easy as it may sound. I accosted a couple of people who, like me, were headed in another direction, further into Mexico. And then (so odd, I thought) I suddenly saw a man I knew: Bill C., the former beau of a good friend in San Francisco; this was especially odd because I had last seen Bill in Barcelona, where we all had dinner at the Ama Lur, the peculiar restaurant that I had recently been reminded of in Oaxaca. I spoke to Bill, who was indeed headed back to San Francisco and would be delighted to be my courier, he said. We then headed off to the bar, to kill more mutual time with margaritas and reminiscences. (His former lady friend, my friend, had since remarried very happily; Bill was moderately happy to hear about all that.)

THE HOTEL in Mérida, where I arrived very late that night, and where, presumably, Janet already was, having flown down from New York that afternoon, was reassuringly pretty and nice. Having chosen it from a guidebook, I was much relieved—partly because this was Janet's first trip to Mexico, I felt more hostess-responsibility along those lines. The building was old, colonial in design, all built around a central courtyard, with pretty tiles and a nice big fountain. And, off to one side, outdoors, a small but very attractive swimming pool. (Janet and I are both dedicated swimmers; our encounter before this one had been at a splendid hotel in Toronto, with an especially good pool.)

At breakfast the following morning, the dining room was full of Americans and Germans, whom the waiters had all placed at a single cluster of tables, no doubt thinking we were all of the same nationality: We were, on the whole, very noisy and elderly travelers (it is astonishing, the number of extremely fat, aging men who wear walking shorts on trips), plus a few serious-looking Yucatán scholars, with beards and backpacks—of all ages, since Mérida is more or less the jumping off place for the Yucatán.

Waiting for Janet, I tried to overhear conversations (my favorite pastime, at breakfast in strange hotels), but I heard nothing that would in any way differentiate this from any other tourist destination, anywhere:

"—this cute little store."

"—really fresh shrimp."

"—no laundry."

And a great deal in German, which I do not understand.

But all of which served to confirm my view that Americans in Mexico make whatever they will of the country.

I first met Janet well over forty years ago, at college, in the forties; we both began at Radcliffe in the summer of forty-three, and though we did not know each other well then, we did take a writing class together, where I was much struck and impressed by her extreme intelligence, her wit, and her wry, slightly slanted perceptions. I still am struck, and impressed, plus she is an enormously good-natured woman—ideal for travel.

After breakfast we went first to a nearby travel agency, where I rapidly found out that the plane I had meant to take on my homeward journey actually did not fly its announced route: a pronouncement that filled me with acute anxiety; already I was thinking too much of my return to D. Also, as the energetic Mexican woman at the agency pointed out, geographically my plan did not make sense: Why return at all to Mérida from San Cristóbal? Why not fly from Tuxtla (near San Cristóbal) back to Mexico City? For God knows what local travel regulatory reasons, she could not, however, make the appropriate ticket adjustments—and I began, then, to find my return trip quite worrying, as though an obstacle course had been placed between me and San Francisco.

Mérida is an extremely pleasant city in which to stroll about. The general effect, as in so much of Mexico, is one of ruined colonial grandeur. Here and there are beautiful, small, pastel-painted houses, splendid with their white columns and formal garlands, their arches and porticoes—obviously once the dwellings of private families, now either some sort of offices, doctors' or lawyers', or fallen into total neglect, a shabby desuetude.

There are many parks and plazas and a beautiful central boulevard, the Paseo Montejo, for serious strolling. In the parks there are white painted S shaped benches, called *confi denciales*, a word that perfectly describes their possible function, that of furnishing space for an intensely confidential conversation. My favorite bandstand, in one of the smaller parks, was also white-painted and consisted of a group of seminaked ladies, vaguely "Greek" in their garb and pose, whose figures supported the curved tin roof. The surrounding trees, too, were painted with lime—and all that whiteness served to lighten the scene.

One's sense is of a busy city, with high employment; the word "bustling" inevitably came to mind, especially in the early mornings, as workers' buses, incredibly old, clattered past our hotel, along with motorcycles and cars, so many cars. "No mufflers is one of the problems," Janet observed, early on. "No mufflers and brand-new horns."

In one of our guidebooks, hitherto highly reliable, we came across this intriguing sentence about Mérida: "Nowhere else in the country, for instance, do you hear so many men giggling." Quite fascinated by this possibility, Janet and I were both alert for giggling men, but we observed none, nowhere— not in restaurants or parks, nor on the streets, nor on the bus that we took to the Museum of Popular Arts. And we wondered: If this is true, and Mérida men indeed do giggle a lot, how did the writer of the guidebook know about it? Where is all this alleged giggling done? In Spanish, *giggle* is expressed by two words, a phrase that literally means "to laugh in a silly way"; I asked the maid in our hotel if many local men did that (feeling very silly myself at the question), and that somewhat somber lady said no, not in her observation.

The Museum of Popular Arts seemed to have at least three addresses; we spent an hour or so circling the same blocks, searching it out—and at last coming upon an inconspicuous entrance that we must have passed several times. It turned out, however, to reward our diligence richly; it is a wonderfully rich museum, well maintained and, seemingly, in constant use by scholars and schoolchildren, as well as stray tourists like ourselves. It contains cases of quite beautiful handmade clothes and some wonderfully witty masks, I thought, of devils (one with a literally forked tongue), pigs, and bearded men. And cases of large skeleton figures in costumes, engaged in homey occupations, like cooking or carpentry. A large skeleton with scary teeth wears a sweet little pink apron and seems to be preparing a small chicken for roasting; another, seated, wears a brown cobbler's apron and is fixing a shoe, with a hammer and nails.

The contrast between the "popular art" found in these many local museums, and its imitations, the thousands of pounds of them all over the stores, is sad and terrible indeed. In the museums themselves, however, there quite often seem to be museum stores, in which certainly not everything is good, but overall the level is much higher than elsewhere, outside.

Janet, with a magazine article to write on crafts in Mexico, had an expense account with which to buy *objets*, to be photographed as illustrations for her article; they, the people at the magazine, wanted her to spend a lot of money, and the problem was that she couldn't find anything that cost enough for them. "It's pretty, but it's just not expensive enough," we said to each other, from time to time.

OFTEN, DURING this visit to Mérida, in the mid- to late afternoons we would come back to our hotel for at least a brief time in our small, cool, stone pool, a relief from the Mérida heat, which was considerable. Happily, the pool seemed to be not much used by the other guests; we generally had it to ourselves. Janet, a very tidy person, became engaged in removing leaves from the pool as she swam, and I, though by nature not especially neat, followed along; the removal of leaves became the sort of easy, mindless, possibly meditative chore that many writers seem to enjoy when not working, I have found.

And at night we tried out various recommended restaurants. I see us alone in a high pale-green room (there is often in Mexico the problem of coming to meals too early), eating what is touted as the finest, most interesting food in Mexico— and not finding it very wonderful. I managed to develop a mild fondness for something called *papa dzules*, which are basically tortillas (I very much like tortillas, fortunately, and am always annoyed by fancy restaurants that make a point of not serving them) and a fondness, too, for *pollo pipíl*, which is chicken in a red-hot sauce.

As we ate, the Mexican version of Muzak played pleasant, half-familiar forties' songs—and I remembered that in Zihuatancjo all we heard were sixties' songs; perhaps popular culture takes longer to make it to Mérida?

SIGHT-SEEING IN Mérida is considerably more rewarding than shopping is; for one thing, destinations are quite logically arrived at, since all the streets are systematically numbered: The odd numbers go east-west; the even north-south, making it very easy to get and to keep your bearings.

One possible source of confusion, though, is the fact that so many streets and buildings are named *Montejo,* that family having been of prime historical importance in Mérida. The first Montejo was Francisco de Montejo, who was, with Cortés, a companion at arms in the 1519 expedition to conquer the Aztecs, in central Mexico. As a reward for his valiant services, Montejo asked for and was granted permission to conquer the Yucatán (such an amazing request, it now would seem—and such breathtaking "permission"). The Yucatán was, of course, the first area of Mexico seen by the Spaniards when they landed there, and Montejo had apparently been taken with the area—as Cortés was not. This conquest, seemingly carried on in a more-or-less discouraged way (he found no treasure and was sorely beset by rains and by illness) by Montejo, lasted about twenty years—contrasted to the scant two years before Aztec capitulation, a comparison dear to the Yucatán-Mayan boosters in Mérida.

On the *zócalo,* in Mérida called the Plaza Mayor is the Palacio Montejo. Until 1980 the Montejo family still owned and for the most part occupied this building. It now belongs to a bank and has been beautifully, meticulously restored. The façade is especially good, and fierce, with its very realistic carvings of conquistadores, who are trampling on Indians—who are also very real, in their downtrodden suffering.

It seems to me that I have seen many churches billed as "the oldest in Mexico": The cathedral in Mérida is now among that number. It is noted for its *Christ of the Blisters*, a wooden statue reputed to have escaped one fire, miraculously, only to receive its blisters in the next. In any case, these blisters are now hard to see, as the figure is high up in the front of the church—which is otherwise fairly plain, with austere stone vaulting and minimal statuary.

Mérida greatly prides itself on its Mayan past. In fact, the word "Mayan" in Mérida denotes high culture, a glorious history. Mayans, according to local legend, were both gentle and brave, as well as vastly talented, and of course possessed of both artistic and scientific genius—unlike the bloody Aztecs (despite the fact that, in the long run, more Spaniards were killed by Mayans than by Aztecs). The excellent Archaeological Museum rather contradicts some aspects of this legend, with its skull collection; the skulls of small children were purposefully deformed by the Mayans to produce the desired long head. Other collections, though, attest to a highly developed culture. Partly because of the sheer length of the Mayan resistance to the Spaniards, in Mérida, more is known of Mayan families than elsewhere, and it is in the anthropology museum that we see relics of those families, their jewels and pottery, their costumes and religious masks.

Even the "modern" murals by Pacheco, in the State Government Palace, have a Mayan emphasis, and a bronze plaque, dated 1971, gives a history of the origin of Mayan man, from the Mayan sacred book, the *Popul Vuh*. (The general idea is that man grew from wheat that was fertilized by wind and stars—which beats certain Fundamentalist ideas, it seems to me.)

The University of Mérida, which was established as a Jesuit college early in the seventeenth century, was just across from our hotel, and I awoke each day to sunlight on bright white Moorish arches, across the way.

All in all, Mérida was a city that I was loath to leave

and one to which I would like to return—in fact, as so much of the rest of the trip became so complicated, I often longed for what increasingly seemed the easy pleasantness of Mérida, and I rather envied Janet, who was, in fact, to end her trip with a couple of more days there—instead of going on to San Cristóbal with Cynthia and me.

MAILING A letter to D. presented the usual challenge—I found no one in the hotel who planned an imminent return to the States, and when I asked at the desk for Mexican stamps, "Ah no," I was told. "Out of stamps." (A condition that seemed to be chronic.)

But, I was further told, the hotel across the street often had stamps, they would surely have stamps today. I walked across the street, thinking (uncharitably) that one of the bus-boys lounging out in front could have done this for me. At that hotel, at the desk, as I asked for a stamp, I was answered by a firm headshake: No, no stamps. But then there was the bright second thought that the gift shop might have stamps. Following directions, I made my way through labyrinthine corridors to the gift shop, a small crowded room (full of the most appalling junk, from the look of it) where, in the farthest back drawer of some chest, a stamp indeed was found. I paid, and affixed the stamp to my letter, and gave it up with some reluctance to the mail slot at the hotel, feeling that I had gone as far as I could go.

And, in fact, the letter never arrived in San Francisco.

HIRING A car and driver has a sound of grandeur that in Mexico is quite misleading. Janet and I hired a car with a driver-guide for the trip from Mérida, via Uxmal, to Campeche, for about 150 dollars, somewhat more than the bus would have been but far, far less than air travel—and the truth about flying anywhere in Mexico is that you generally cannot go from one city to another without going back to Mexico City, which is often geographically crazy. We set off, then, with our luggage and our driver—Luís, a stolid adolescent with a scruffy, incipient mustache and a large, aggressive stock of information. Before we were out of Mérida he was pounding into our ears what we already knew about Montejo's conquest of the Yucatán.

Luís managed to inject heavy reverence into each sounding of the small word "Mayan"—and he used that word at least five or six times in each sentence.

And what he said was all very interesting, but we had already read it all ourselves; and in the assertive, monotonous voice of Luís it was hard indeed to bear. Even apart from the "M." word, Luís was very given to didactic phrases: "you must"—"you can prove"—"you will find"—"you have to understand." All very aggressive and unpleasant. (I should admit that I often do not do well with guides, though, or for that matter with many, if not most, forms of instruction.)

Now, thinking back to my considerable (and, I am afraid, ill-concealed) impatience with him, I see the fairly small and relatively controlled beginning of a most unprecedented war—between myself and various Mexicans whom in one way or another I hired to help me, the mighty tourist with dollars. This impatience finally (and humiliatingly) extended itself to maids in hotels—about all that more later. At the time I only thought that Luís was too annoying to listen to. Janet seemed less impatient with him than I did, but she is both a better student and a better-natured person than I am.

The drive itself, though, once we had calmed Luís down somewhat, was interesting. Janet, who had spent time in India and Africa, remarked that it looked to her very much like India: low furze, odd, rounded, thatched huts (one of my guidebooks had described these as the marks of the Yucatán). Chickens and cows all over. The cows looked especially Indian, said Janet.

At various crossroads, as Luís stopped our car, clusters of children would crowd around, selling what looked to be orange juice. We were hot and thirsty, and the drink looked very cool and good, and the children with their large, brown, sad eyes were very appealing; still, middle-class Americans to the core, we forebore. It was just the stuff to make us very sick, we believed. After several such encounters I developed a curious delusion, which was that I was seeing the same small boy repeatedly—at every stop he was there, to be disappointed, repeatedly, by me.

Uxmal, our first ruin, flourished from A.D. 600 to 900 and is an example of late Mayan architecture (or Puuc, named for the surrounding hills). It is believed to have been built by people from the cities of Palenque, Jaina, and Bonampak, who, abandoning their own centers (for reasons not entirely clear), moved northward. After Uxmal was built, it was invaded by a tribe called the Itzas, whose worship was Toltec and whose finest city was Chichén Itzá. In the twelfth and thirteenth centuries there was a coalition government—Uxmal, Chichén Itzá, and Mayapán—and several centuries of peace, a truce; followed by more wars, and the virtual extinction of the aesthetic achievement that had flourished under both the Mayans and the Toltecs. By the fifteenth century there was little activity of any nature among the Mayans and Toltecs—and in the sixteenth century the luxuriant jungle surrounding Uxmal was destroyed by fire.

The area is still scrubby looking (it seems very strange that the jungle has not grown back, in all that time); it is intimidatingly large and bare on a very hot day. There are, however, several groups of magnificently, intricately constructed buildings, of what seemed an extreme steepness. And Luís told us that each year several people were killed there. "They just fall down," he rather stolidly pointed out, as though this were a reasonably (perhaps Mayan) sacrifice. I could all too easily imagine their "just falling," and I decided, as I had all along known would be the case, not to climb anything.

Luís guided us into some remarkable enclosed courtyards, all ornamented with extraordinary friezes—mostly of snakes, snakes in many avatars and guises. "But all snakes. The Mayans were fond of snakes. Very important," Luís told us.

For some reason (there must have been a tour group of them), on the day that Janet and I visited Uxmal there were a large number of disabled people, with degrees of handicap ranging from those barely making it on heavy crutches to those confined in motorized chairs. It was a little hard not to sentimentalize their sheer guts (to contrast them with one's own), for they looked to be quite genuinely brave, and serious, and happy, exploring and climbing—indeed, clambering about: Several of that group managed to scramble up the steep sides of a pyramid, despite warning signs—and happily, there were no falls or injuries that day.

In part to escape from Luís and his Mayan panegyrics, Janet and I began to follow a small country road that led, so the signs informed us, toward the Temple of the Old Woman. The road was gentle and winding, of yellow clay; it looked much like the country roads of my North Carolina childhood. And Janet, because I had known her for so long, could almost have been a friend from that time. Which led to conversations that the actual circumstances render somewhat odd:

"Whatever happened to Carol Coatsworth, do you ever hear?"

"*Well*, odd that you should ask. Remember she had all those children? Five or six, I never could get it straight, but a lot. And the husband that no one liked, no one but Carol. He taught at Duke, which I hear is quite good for a southern school—"

"Not really. And Nixon went there, didn't he?"

"I think. And Carol's husband taught something strange, like business administration. Anyway, all the kids turned out very well indeed, unscathed by Duke, or the sixties, all doing satisfactory things like grad schools or high-class crafts. And then suddenly Carol went back to school. Not Duke, but up to Yale, for a master's in anthropology. And then guess what, off to Africa to study some tribe—"

"Divorcing what's-his-name?"

"I think, eventually. But she couldn't be happier, everyone says."

And so on.

The road led on and on. At a certain point we remarked, "How interesting to be lost in Uxmal," and then we walked on, as Janet told me about her life in India, how everything they ate had to be washed and boiled.

And then, having almost decided that we were in fact lost and should really turn around, we saw a tiny sign, saying again THE TEMPLE OF THE OLD WOMAN, and an arrow pointing off into a field where, at what looked to be a considerable distance, we made out a very small, unprepossessing house. No point in continuing, we thought, and did not.

We turned back and eventually were reunited with Luís, who seemed not to have worried about us, and who then deposited us in a restaurant near the ruins—which was awful, and which we we almost immediately abandoned in favor of the only other restaurant, which Luís had said was no good. (He was right, but his recommendation may well have been terrible too.)

WE STOPPED for gas at a place that Luís said was of great interest: A wild pig in captivity was there. Not dying to see a wild pig, but rather feeling that we must, we passed through a very large store crammed with cases of souvenirs, routine silver and gold filagree, and racks and racks of machine-embroidered clothes—and out to a small, enclosed backyard, with spindly trees and unsuccessful flowers, and a very small wire-fenced enclosure, where, indeed, there was a tiny, very hairy, long-snouted pig. Who, if indeed he was wild, gave us no visible or audible signs of wildness.

CAMPECHE

Campeche was originally called "Ah Kim Pech" and was a Mayan village. Then, under Charles III (in the mid-eighteenth century), it was called "The City of San Francisco de Campeche," and then more or less ignored. Approaching its outskirts, one can see why. It is nowhere near being the pretty little seaside resort that was in our minds as we three had made our reservations.

The first visible sign of Campeche was a block of tiny (dollhouse-size) model homes in various pastel shades, in what looked to be perfect plastic. All finished and waiting, not one occupied or sold. In fact, it is impossible to imagine the sort of Mexican or tourist family that could possibly fit themselves into those miniature spaces: Where would the spare shoes go? The boys' and girls' toys? The father's hat? Not to mention the fat grandmother who had paid for the trip? The whole development seemed one of those monstrously bad ideas that one expects to vanish overnight, as certain concepts are discarded by one's mind, and some bad dreams forgotten.

A very old-looking sign announced A VENDRE, a further puzzle: Why on earth in French? Surely the often practical and often tasteful French people would be the first to recognize such a very bad idea.

A CERTAIN problem with reservations in Campeche had arisen in the months before this trip—and actually it is surprising that there was not more trouble, given the situation of three separate travel agents, in three very far-apart cities. The upshot of this trouble was that I could not get into the hotel I had chosen for the three of us, whereas both Janet from New York and Cynthia from Chicago were easily booked. This worried me a little: Suppose the two of them did not get along and the hotels were far apart? However, as we approached Janet's hotel, where Cynthia, presumably, already was, with Luís at the wheel, I saw that the two hotels were almost adjacent to each other.

Both buildings faced the sea, across a seaside boulevard that was singularly devoid of attractiveness—as was the sea, just there. Flat and oily, that ocean looked polluted; there were no swimmers anywhere along that stretch, and very few small boats. It was altogether emphatically uninviting.

My room in the hotel (that I had not wanted) was small but adequate, with a sea-directed window that afforded a better view than one got at actual sea level. And since the general look of the hotel suggested that there were no superior rooms, I settled in, more or less.

By the time I got across to the other hotel, the supposedly more desirable one, for drinks before dinner with Cynthia and

Janet, as we had arranged, they had already met (this meeting that I had worried about took place offstage, so to speak) and were passionately united in their dislike of that hotel. Their rooms were dirty (both are women of great fastidiousness), and the elevator stopped between floors and opened its door to black coils and terrifying black space. There was no hot water.

Cynthia though a very soft-spoken woman, is more intense than Janet is; Janet, in many ways a New Englander, tends to make the best of things, to adjust. And so it was Cynthia who said, "Well, thank God we're leaving on Sunday."

"Not till Monday," I reminded her (I had been the master planner of all this travel, after all).

"No, I'm sure it's Sunday, the seventh."

"No, Monday, the eighth."

"I have Monday, the eighth, too, for leaving," put in Janet.

I still do not see quite how or why this confusion, this contradiction of dates took place, but nevertheless it had: Janet and I were booked to leave Campeche and drive to Palenque on Monday the eighth and Cynthia on Sunday the seventh. There was no possible reason for this. Also, we had as yet no driver for either day.

All of this involved a great deal of discussion, over bad drinks, there in the bad hotel bar. Because of her strange flight schedule from Chicago, Cynthia had been there for thirty-six hours already, she was very, very anxious to leave ("This place is truly awful."), and she had found a man whom she thought could be our driver. He was to meet us in the bar, where we were. (Bar: a terrible small room that could be more accurately described as a TV lounge, with garish plaid-covered overstuffed furniture, blaring staticky sound, and a screen full of angry faces. I could see why Cynthia was so eager to leave that hotel.)

Since we seemed unclear as to the date of our departure, there seemed little point in talking to a prospective driver; however, there he suddenly was, a small, dark, shifty-eyed man in a light, thin, shabby suit—a man who smiled too much and never looked at our faces as we talked. And we spent what seemed like several hours with him. Juan. In that bar.

The upshot—insofar as there was an upshot—was his offer to drive us to Palenque for $150. On Sunday. He could not do it in Monday.

Various emotions emerged in response to this, all conflicting, and in the course of discussion these emotions grew more heated. Cynthia passionately wanted to leave, to get out of there on Sunday. Janet, a more moderate and thrifty person, thought we might get a better deal somewhere else: Why rush into this one? (It was Friday night.) I simply wanted to get the whole thing settled, I did not much care how. However, my Cuernavaca experience with drivers had led me to believe that indeed there always was another driver.

Cynthia became increasingly anxious to get rid of Juan so that we could (we hoped) arrive at our own decisions, and at last she said to him, "You must leave now, so that my friends and I can decide what to do." But still he hung around for another ten minutes or so, as though he feared that left to our own (surely untrustworthy) devices, we would come to some decision that was contrary to his interests.

At last he took off, and from the desk we called for a taxi (Janet's magazine had told her about a good restaurant in Campeche). We went outside, where we were faced with a vast and empty parking lot—where we waited, and waited, and waited. And were finally told that no taxis were coming, there were no taxis.

150

THE NEXT day was better all around—beginning, from my room, with a lovely dawn over the sea: rippling gentle water and beautiful, pale, delicate clouds, a breeze in the palm fronds around the hotel pool.

Down in the dining room I found Cynthia in a state of some excitement. She had called Chicago from my hotel and had got very good news of her show: eight paintings already sold (eight out of seventeen after only three days seemed very good indeed) and rumors of a forthcoming very good review in the *Tribune*. "I hate to miss all the excitement there," she told me.

"But won't it still be going on when you get back?"

"Not exactly. The momentum gets lost."

We had arranged to meet Janet at the travel agent's desk at my hotel, but by the time of the meeting Cynthia was eager to be off and painting. "You two arrange it. I'll do anything. Just get me out of here."

And so Janet and I arranged with the travel agent, Miguel, a mere boy, to change our reservations to a day earlier in Palenque. And to be picked up by a driver the next day, Sunday morning.

In the meantime, Janet and I set out to explore Campeche; Cynthia had given us directions to her garden, her temporary painting area. "I don't think you'll find a great deal to see in the town," she told us. "To me it looks like a Soviet resort in Israel." (Thus reconfirming my view that people, even highly sophisticated travelers, like Cynthia, tend to make odd projections onto Mexico—although for all I know Campeche does indeed look like a Soviet resort in Israel.)

Janet and I agreed, though, with Cynthia's verdict. "It

looks like upstate New York," Janet said. "One wonders where the fancy stores and houses are. Where do the rich people live, or are there any rich?"

If there are no visible rich people in Campeche today, there certainly were in the sixteenth and seventeenth centuries, the greatest source of wealth being timber from the surrounding (now-vanished) forests; an expensive and rare red dye was made from the wood and exported as far as England, where it was used for the coats of uniforms. Thus, pirates were strongly attracted to the city—siege after bloody siege was endured; at one time there were eight sets of fortifications, all but one of which remain. And several of which Janet and I explored, along with a couple of local museums that are mostly concerned with the history of wars against the pirates, with guns and gun emplacements—not of great interest to either of us.

We inspected the dusty, neglected *zócalo* and the Cathedral of Saint Bartholomew, which was finished in 1546 and is the oldest church on the Yucatán peninsula. It is interesting in that the local workers seem to have had less specifically Spanish directions than usual: All the faces portrayed look distinctly Mayan (with the strange, long flat noses and heavy mouths), especially on all the faces of the Stations of the Cross.

IN THE course of our aimless strolling, along what we took to be the main streets of Campeche, we passed an open booth at which the Salk vaccine was being handed out, children lined up with their mothers to receive the small sugar cubes, like communion. What was interesting was that the kids screamed as though they were actually getting shots, of the old-fashioned kind, instead of sugar.

The stores were full of the usual mix—of essentially nothing. Wedding dresses predominated, all flounced and laced, often with white pearl embroidery for the brides and yards of pastel flounces for the maids of honor—all, to North American eyes, like visions from the thirties, and all quite unwearable, conceivably, for other occasions. There is, I suppose, the fact that in such a Catholic country one wedding would probably be it; neither parents nor participants would expect to go through all that severe expense twice. Still, it does seem onorous, and the emphasis does seem a little off.

Having done fortifications, as it were, we set out to find the garden where Cynthia had said she would be painting.

Which we did, and we came upon a very strange sight indeed: a small rock garden that included a pool and some somnolent goldfish, lots of tropical plants. And Cynthia, in her bikini and round straw hat, with easel and painting equipment. And—a wedding: bride and groom and attendants, and their photographer.

As I should have said earlier, Cynthia is very striking, beautiful, really: a tall thin blonde with exotic large dark-blue eyes (she is distantly Polish, I think).

The bride and groom were both small and dark, and young, most painfully young; they looked about seventeen, but I hope they were at least a few years older. They looked very sweet and bewildered, seeming to have very little notion that an event of far-reaching consequences was taking place. From time to time they stole glances at Cynthia, as though she were some divine intervening visitor who might furnish them with necessary clues to life. Cynthia, as always when she works, was totally absorbed in her project.

THE NEXT morning I woke to a power failure in my hotel. No air-conditioning, scant water, no lights. I went down to breakfast with limited expectations, to say the least, but the management had, surprisingly, come through: Some sort of stove had been able to provide toast and coffee, and there was plenty of good fresh fruit. *Mexico.*

At the table next to mine an American, a man in late middle age with steely gray hair and heavy, reddish features, was haranguing his breakfast companions, Mexican men, about life in Miami (and I fell into my old habit of breakfast eavesdropping). "It's got its faults," he told them. "We have some problems, but we're very comfortable there. Whereas here, here it's all poor management. You've got the facilities, but there's too much paper here. Forms. Everything requires a couple of dozen permissions." And then, to the waiter, "This toast is too soft. I want it cooked more. More hard. Dry. It's too *soft.*"

Midbreakfast, abruptly, all the lights came on, along with the very loud rumble of the air conditioner.

A few minutes after that, the American from Miami was summoned to the phone. Looking important, he dashed his napkin to the table and hurried off—but came back very soon, looking inquiringly at me.

"Your name Adams?"

"Yes—"

"Call's for you. Don't know how they got it confused."

Nor did I know, and I would rather not think about what the people at the desk thought we had in common, description-wise, we two gringos.

But the call was indeed for me, and it was from D., whom I had missed a lot—which I managed to say, or rather to shout; the phone was almost in the middle of the lobby.

OUR DRIVER was to meet us promptly at 10:00, and promptly at 10:00 there appeared the boy–travel

agent who was to be our driver, Miguel. He had brought along
another boy, his cousin, he said, to keep him company on the
drive, and especially on the drive back from Palenque when he
would be very tired. Janet and Cynthia and I expressed in
unison our dismay: The car was very small; we three are all
tall women. There was barely room in the car for four people
and luggage (Cynthia travels with a very large picture tube).
The upshot was that the cousin departed, and we four set off
for Palenque, with Cynthia, the tallest, in the front seat next to
Miguel—who drove very fast indeed, as though angrily trying
to eat up the miles to Palenque, to diminish a five-hour trip. I
was, in fact, more than a little worried about his anger—in
part, of course, because I felt it was justified; it would have
been nicer for him to have a return-trip companion. I was half-
afraid that he might just dump us off somewhere—three
robbed and dead American women, an ugly news item, somewhere. Two writers, one painter.

The landscape, as we left the coast and headed into the
interior, was quite marvelous: increasingly lush and green,
with wide, flat rivers to cross and meadows full of large
strange birds, and cows with curious humps.

We all felt reassured as small signs began to point toward
Palenque, and we even began to see signs that specifically
advertised our hotel; we were going in the right direction after
all and probably were not going to be killed and left in a ditch.
We were slightly disconcerted, though, as, on our actual approach to the town, it became clear that Miguel had never
been there before (he had said that he had made this trip
many times), but at last we came to a crossroads with signs
that pointed in one direction to *Ruinas* and in the other to
our hotel.

After parting from Miguel, and after some confusion and
skirmishes with the very pretty Indian girls who were in
charge at the front desk (they had not received any messages

from Miguel, now departed, in his guise as travel agent, and did not know that we were to come a day earlier), we were shown to our rooms, the three of them in a row, strung out along a walkway that overlooked a large lawn, and then looked out to a far green plain, with more birds and white cows, in clusters. And then a range of sharp blue mountains.

Almost immediately below our rooms was a huge, huge tree, spread out like a giant fan against the sky. On one of the lowest branches a skinny old monkey perched and swung his tail down; he was attached to the branch by a long frayed rope. On the ground below the tree was the monkey's house, very small, and his food pail, and a little platform—for showing off on, we came to see.

I loved my room. It was narrow and clean and highly functional, the sort of room in which, after unpacking, I always begin to imagine a more spare, stripped-down existence than the one I now enjoy (and complain about the complications of). What I mostly meant was that it was clearly a place where I could work, I thought. And that turned out to be true; I very much liked working at that table in Palenque—aside from certain problems that later emerged, mostly having to do with noise.

Janet and I decided to try for lunch—Cynthia, who eats rarely and little, went off to paint.

On the way to the dining room we passed a nice large swimming pool—very inviting, except that at the moment a volleyball net was stretched across it, and the pool was full of French people, undoubtedly a tour group of some sort, who were very energetically and very loudly at play, with loud French cries. They were still there when we came back from lunch, but we went swimming anyway, dodging in and out among the French, giving them disapproving looks. Trip presents from D. had been a small flashlight and a little knife; I now imagined going out to the pool at midnight and cutting down the net. I might also liberate the monkey, while I was at it.

Cynthia had settled herself near the base of the tree, near the monkey and his perch—in her bikini and round straw hat, with her big easel and paints. A couple of loose parrots had arrived from somewhere, as though to inspect—and that is one of my permanent memories of Palenque, that picture of the lovely giant tree, with the painter and the monkey near its base. And those parrots. And far in the background that marvelous, mysterious green plain, with its clusters of cows, and birds.

Before taking a nap that afternoon I put up the DO NOT DISTURB—*NO MOLESTAR* sign, but just as I had fallen off (of course), there was a loud knock, and I opened the door to see a maid with a list: Every day at this time it was necessary that she count the guests, she told me. I pointed to the sign, which indicated my presence, I would have thought; she repeated that she had to count the guests. This exchange marked the beginning of a war that was to last for the length of our stay— so vile and degrading, to develop an antipathy for a maid, but I did. I entirely disliked this woman, her pale powdered skin and her painted-on eyebrows, her small, hostile, unintelligent eyes.

I AM not sure yet why we put off going to the ruins at Palenque, but we did. Perhaps it seemed so momentous that we needed to be prepared in some way, like the preparations that some people used to make for acid trips. Instead, Janet and I set off the next morning for town, as though we were in a perfectly ordinary place, as though there were nothing highly remarkable in the neighborhood.

The town of Palenque, which has simply grown up as

more and more tourists have come to visit, has the look of a frontier town in an old western movie: mostly one-story stucco buildings, dirty and shabby, and streets that are either unpaved or covered with broken slabs of concrete. Garbage in the gutters. Stores, restaurants, and bars—all more or less open to the street. Some very druggy-looking North American kids, scruffy and skinny, all sitting together on the sidewalk. And a very plain, unassuming church: Franciscan, from the look of it, with nice rows of red-painted wrought-iron benches out in front.

Having cased the town, in a leisurely walk, we headed back for the most promising-looking store. Janet still needed some props for her magazine article, and I needed—nothing. But I always look for funny earrings for certain Texas friends and for one elegant Napa Valley friend. And the shop indeed was very nice, with some genuinely good handmade clothes and artifacts, some local and some from Guatemala, which is very nearby.

As we indecisively picked up and put down the various objects that struck us in one way or another, a woman in khaki clothes came in, and she too looked at a couple of skirts, a blouse—and everything about her informed us that although she was clearly North American she lived there, she was less a tourist than a resident of Palenque.

And so it turned out. Martha, a biologist from Delaware, was a part-time (four months a year) resident of Palenque and had been there for more than twenty years. We found this out over a delicious drink to which she introduced us—after rudimentary introductions we had asked her if she would come out for coffee with us. A *liquado de piña con hielo y agua purificado*—pineapple juice with ice and purified water (it loses a lot in translation, I think).

Martha, like many longtime residents anywhere, was fond of telling us how much her chosen place had declined;

we should have come to Palenque twenty years ago, she said, when they all (all the investigating scientists, I guess) used to have picnics at night among the ruins. Before all the terrible thefts of artifacts had become so prevalent. Martha had a friend, an anthropologist, who was murdered: She, the friend, had happened on a group of thieves in a hitherto unexplored Mayan temple, and they had stabbed her, killing her, horribly.

Martha also had two very useful practical suggestions: She knew a very good travel agency that would take care of our homeward problems (I still had no clear ticket to San Francisco and still often thought of D. with longing); she also knew of a very good local restaurant.

The travel agency, to which we three went the next day, was excellent: Janet was to fly from Villahermosa back to Mérida, as she wished. And Cynthia and I were to fly from Tuxtla Gutiérrez to Mexico City; we would hire cars between Palenque and San Cristóbal and from San Cristóbal to Mexico City. I was, in fact, so pleased with the finality of a ticket, an actual ticket connecting me to Mexico City and thus to San Francisco (and to D.), that I overpaid by about $100—which the travel agent returned to me with apologies: He should have noticed my error right away, he said.

And the restaurant to which we went that night with Martha was very good, an interestingly built large structure patterned on the small round straw huts, with a very high (about three stories high) woven ceiling.

WAKING IN Palenque, in my narrow room, was marvelous: Before dawn there were broad streaks of silver dew across the grass and purple mists over the mountains. A gold blur of sun, slowly rising.

The monkey lay in a heap on the ground, all bundled up.

He could have been dead, but then, as slowly as a dancer rising, he got up and began to scratch, then picked up an old banana, and peeled and ate it.

THE NEXT good thing that happened was that the French tour group departed, all those ardent volleyball players, so that we had hopes of a decent swim.

And: After breakfast we took the jitney bus out to the ruins. We would do this every day, we decided. Like going to the Prado every day that you're in Madrid.

The entrance to the ruins is bad, given over to a long bazaar and an unattractive restaurant-bar. And to tour buses, lined up all over the area, disgorging the dutifully curious along with serious scholars, Germans and Japanese, French and North Americans. If you did not arrive with a tour, as we did not, great efforts were made to line you up with one, efforts that Janet and I resisted, adamantly.

Once we had cleared all that and walked out toward the great green space where the ruins stand, with the powerful dark green jungle rising all around, we were quite overcome: It is marvelous.

Most striking, perhaps most beautiful, at first, are the colors: the black-gray-white of the ancient carved and weathered stones, and all the contrasting greens, the light green grass and dark trees, with every shade of green in-between, in bushes and vines and smaller trees. And then your eye returns to the ruins and you think again, How very beautiful, simply, the stones are.

Not everyone is so affected. Here speaks Graham Greene:

> I haven't been to Chichén Itzá, but judging from the photographs of the Yucatán remains they are immeasurably more impressive than those of Palenque, though, I suppose, if you

like wild nature, the setting of Palenque is a finer one—on a
great circular plateau half-way up the mountainside, with the
jungle falling precipitously below into the plain and rising
straight up behind. . . . And no shade anywhere until you've
climbed the steep loose slopes and bent inside the dark cool
little rooms like lavatories where a few stalactites have
formed. . . . (*Lawless Roads,* 140)

(This sounds much more like Greene-land than Palenque
to me.)

Janet and I wandered, feckless and unencumbered by
archaeological information; we agreed that it would be more
fun to see the ruins and then study them later, at home (which
is more or less what I have done). We climbed around like
children, among the serious French tourist-scholars—up and
down stone structures, down into caves and tunnels. Once we
even felt somewhat lost (until I brought out my trusty flashlight, the present from D.), and Janet said, "Well, it's not a
real adventure unless we get lost."

And we continued our endless, labyrinthine conversations.

J: "Of all the men you knew, who did you love most, do
you think?"

A: "Well, X. I guess. That's why I stayed with him for
so long."

J: "Have you written about him?"

A: "No, but I will. Sometime. I guess. And you, who did
you care most about?"

J: "Oh. Y. Absolutely. I was so terrifically proud of him."

Walking a little back into the jungle reminded me (again)
of walks in the woods around Chapel Hill, as had the woods
around Uxmal. And I wondered if in some sense all journeys
are returns to some earlier imagining. All those years ago,
when I was small and looked up to great festoons of honey-
suckle vines, I thought of Tarzan movies, and jungles—so

that now, as a much taller person, I looked at the jungles of Palenque, in Mexico, and I referred them back to those earlier versions of jungle.

THE POOL indeed became ours, wonderful to come back to after walking in the heat (the jungle heat). There were always a couple of other guests around, with whom I often seemed to fall into conversation.

A small, fat, and visibly exhausted woman, whose husband slept and snored in a deck chair, dangled her feet in the water, so nice and cool, and told me that she was on a twenty-three-day rail tour of Mexico, where she had not been before. "Except, you know, when you stop for a day of cruises."

I wondered: Do I look like the sort of person who goes on cruises? I'm afraid that I must.

She was not going out to see the ruins, she said. "I've seen a lot of them this trip, and I'm not that much into ruins."

I talked to a young couple from Michigan, on the other hand, who were very much into ruins. "I'm a ruins freak," the young man said. "Vietnam, Cambodia, anywhere there's ruins. My favorites are at Khartoum, but they're being wrecked like everything else, with that goddamn dam, the Aswan."

He also said that he loved the nightlife in Palenque. I pushed that further, unable to imagine what he could have meant, and he told me, "The popcorn! Popcorn stands! It's not like home, not real fluffed out, but it's popcorn."

THAT AFTERNOON the weather got hotter yet, and more still. Ocher-gray clouds began to cover the sky, very dark, getting darker, over the mountains. In the giant tree the leaves all trembled, and the monkey rushed up and down his rope, in a frenzy. Then, across that dark ocher sky, there were long, brilliant, crooked lines of lightning, and heavy thunder roared. Out on the plain the white cows all huddled together. Lashing winds came up, and then the rain, beating the palm fronds, the bamboo and bougainvillea. The monkey huddled in his house, as more lightning flashed, along with more wind, and rain.

Almost as soon as it began the storm was over, then, and flights of great white birds rose up from the plain, and very slowly the white cows began to disperse, to venture out in the long tall grass.

THE ROOM-COUNTING maid bangs loudly on my door.

If I were not here, I tell her, I would not have been able to put out the *No Molestar* sign.

She smiles, malevolently. She must count everyone, she tells me, and points to her list.

INSIDE MY room's phone directory were very clear instructions for calling the States. A certain set of numbers and preferred hours were given. It was easier, according to the instructions, to dial directly, station-to-station. I dialed all those numbers, having calculated a time when D. would most likely be at home (he lives alone). I got nothing, no reasonable, comprehensible sound. I tried several times and then gave up and went out to the desk to ask why my call wasn't going through.

Oh, impossible to dial direct. Better to call collect.

But (I am not sure why I felt so strongly about this at the time) I preferred not to call collect. I wanted to make a station-to-station call, and pay for it.

In that case I must pay $50.

No.

Reviewing this scene, I do wonder at my own stubborn refusal to make the call collect, since later on, in Tuxtla, I did precisely that, several times. Nor do I see why or how the exchange became so heated, so unpleasant. But heated and very unpleasant it did indeed become. I felt, as I had with the maid with her list, that I was being deliberately blocked and confronted with total unreason, if not with malice. And I was shocked and surprised by that feeling.

DIRECTLY IN front of our hotel lay the road into town; turning off to the left, though, was a winding, true country road, out into farmland. From there one could see the marvelous tree—beneath which, invisible from that distance, the monkey gamboled and Cynthia sat painting. And one could see too the distant plain, where the strange white cows and the flocks of herons lived.

I walked out there several times, usually encountering people—once a sort of vagrant, he looked to be, with a load of wood and old shoes on his back; at other times mothers with several small children. We all exchanged brief greetings, but mostly they all stared at such a strange person, a tall woman with very gray hair, wearing pants and silver earrings.

JANET AND I went to visit Martha, in her small house up in some woods. A house crammed with books and small statues, pictures, everywhere engravings and photographs. The engravings were especially interesting to me, in that they were mostly nineteenth-century renditions of Mexican ruins, and all the artists had imposed their own backgrounds: There were Greek, Italian, and Hudson Valley "ruins," further proof, I thought, of my notion that we all impose our own preconceptions on Mexico.

The disintegration and loss of archaeological artifacts is a severe and very sad problem in Mexico, Martha told us. Mostly through theft, but they have also suffered great losses from acid rain and from the sun. She pointed to her own store of artifacts, several bookshelves full. "Of course I got these before owning them or taking them out of the country was illegal, and now I don't quite know what to do with them."

Even eight years ago, Martha told us, it was much harder to get from the town out to the ruins, and thus, she implied, the ruins used to look much better than they did now.

NEVERTHELESS, JANET and I continued to think, on our daily excursions out there, on the nice, reliable jitney, that the ruins were vastly beautiful and of enormous interest.

Early explorers, enthralled both by the beauty of the buildings and the treasures therein, rather wildly estimated that the whole city took up a space of sixty square miles. More recent, slightly calmer estimates put the size at dimensions considerably smaller, maybe five miles wide, two long. But in any case, the area involved is enormous and mostly still unexplored. And these days one feels that it most likely never will be; further exploration of Palenque must be low on the list of priorities in the currently near-disaster Mexican economy.

There is the lovely stone, some beautiful bas-relief

carvings still more or less intact, in the inner courtyards—though much has been hacked off by thieves, brutally. Or even by scholars. And there is the jungle. The two forces seem to approach each other, perhaps in a sort of marriage rite: the ruins and the jungle.

Most recent excavations were financed by the Rockefeller Foundation, a phase that was then called off by the Mexican government, which did not (and does not) have enough money to continue the work itself.

"DO YOU remember Binnie Cowan?" Janet asked me. "Well, you know she's a judge now, but she had a tremendous undergraduate affair with _____" (naming a well-known writer). "Before he was famous, of course. Well, he had a heart attack in a taxi and thought he was dying. His publisher was with him in the cab, and he said to the publisher, 'Tell Binnie Cowan I still love her, will you?' Isn't that a romantic story?"

"Very. But he didn't die—"

"No, and of course the publisher told everyone he could think of. The wife was hardly pleased."

"Binnie was, though?"

"Oh, I guess. If she ever heard the story."

THE TEMPLE of the Inscriptions, nearest at hand as we entered the cleared area, was where each day we spent most time. There it was, so tall and beautifully imposing. And its history is both vivid and macabre: Tablets put its date of construction at A.D. 692. Palenque was one of the most important and magnificent cities of what is known as the old Mayan

Empire, Late Classic Period (A.D. 500–800). And discovered within this temple were extraordinarily beautiful funerary objects, jade and pearls, and ceramics—along with five or six skeletons, presumably young men who were sacrificed as guardians to an important, probably older person, to be found within. And indeed he was found, in a crypt held down with very heavy stone.

A STREAM runs across the open clearing, which was formerly an aqueduct—in which early explorers were said to have slept, to avoid the mosquitos.

O NE OF the joys of exploring Palenque on your own is that of walking up into the woods and looking back down at the spread of temples, the beautiful stone. One feels oneself indeed an explorer, one has at least a little sense of how that must have felt, first for the Spanish followers of Cortés, later for the voluble American John Lloyd Stephens and for Frederick Catherwood, the English artist. What I mostly thought, though, as Janet and I stood up there, looking down, was how much I should like to come back here—and with that wish came the somewhat frightened question: How much more would have been uncovered by then, and how much destroyed?

W E MET Martha in town for a final *licuado*, on the day before we were to leave. All over the *zócalo* that day were picketers, with signs reading LIBRE PALENQUE.

Martha explained that this was a case of Indians against the mayor, who had clearly exploited them, had never listened to their interests.

Martha told us too about the eruption of a volcano, fifty miles away. First, bits of ash were noticed on cars that arrived in town; and then, that night, as Martha went for a walk, she noted that all the stars had gone out, no starlight. And then, in the midst of an unnatural stillness, a terrific rumble began, and the huge dark cloud of soot and ash arrived, several feet of ash all over, everywhere—impossible to get rid of, it was there for days. Many people were killed, Martha said, suffocated in their homes. But this fact, being bad for tourism, was never reported—just as, supposedly, the mortality figures of the eighty-five earthquake were greatly reduced, for public (tourist) consumption.

Many cars in Palenque, we noticed that day, bore stickers that said, "The tourist is your friend, treat him well." No wonder, we thought, that many Mexicans feel suffocated with us, do not feel that we are friends, and do not treat us well, but resentfully.

Walking down the now-familiar road to our hotel, we saw black birds circling above, like pieces of soot on a current.

THE NEXT day Janet left early with her driver for Villahermosa, thence to take the plane for Mérida. And, somewhat later that morning, our driver arrived to take Cynthia and me to San Cristóbal de las Casas.

The scenery was not immediately remarkable, and so we talked; we began to discuss our annoyances with the maids, with the help generally, in the hotel that we had just left. A topic that we both found very disturbing.

"Mine woke me up every afternoon."

"Mine stood outside my room and yelled at the monkey."

"Do you think they just couldn't stand us?"

"Maybe. Careless, rich North Americans. That's how we must look. I wouldn't blame them."

"It's probably the hotel's fault, too. A big chain comes in and hires locals and doesn't take time to train them properly."

THE DRIVE to San Cristóbal was, for the most part, quite beautiful. This was February, and the land had very much the look of spring: apple trees in bloom, and here and there on the surrounding slopes, bountiful crystal waterfalls. The shapes of these mountains were strange and wonderful, so sharp and unexpected, so near; we were often separated from a nearby mountain by the narrowest, deepest valley. No point even thinking about the dangers involved, I decided— and I thought instead about the island of Madeira and a marvelous day drive I once had there, the extreme beauty also overwhelming the perils—although on that trip, in Madeira, I was with R., whose driving I entirely trusted. Whereas this young Mexican was totally unknown and might conceivably want to kill us. At the start of the trip Cynthia had several times chided him, "Please slow down," in her gentle voice, and now he seemed reconciled to our conservative wishes.

We passed a very small village of upright wooden huts, not round and thatched but more like tiny, very primitive cabins. No one was around at all, and we assumed that all the inhabitants were off at work, some labor, or extracting food from their surroundings, the women very likely carrying their babies with them.

And we passed fields of corn, and banks of red clay—for me more reminders of North Carolina, which I still think of as home.

OUR ARRIVAL in San Cristóbal, though, was unpropitious. Near its outer walls, an area of ugly garages,
sleazy stores, Cynthia began to mutter, "I can't paint here, I
know I can't." One thing that she meant was, I knew, that it
was extremely cold—heavy dark clouds hung all over the
town. I had been warned about cold, and so had Cynthia, but
unimaginatively, we had both chosen to pay no heed to such
warnings. Also, the town looked so enclosed, all walled, with
small, narrow, winding streets. But: "We'll feel better in our
nice hotel," I told Cynthia. "So interesting, we're staying in
the same place where Graham Greene stayed."

It was indeed where Graham Greene had stayed, the
same Hotel Español—and thus he describes his arrival: "We
had had fourteen hours of riding before we rode into the little
flowery patio of the hotel. A room and a bed with sheets, a
beautifully cooked meal, steak and greens and sweet bread, a
bottle of beer and the radio playing; I was drunk and dazed
with happiness." (*Lawless Roads,* 172) Perhaps those hours
of riding had rendered him grateful; I can only say that our
arrival was quite other, was, in fact, more like the arrival of
Isabella Linton at Wuthering Heights, as Heathcliffe's most
unwelcome wife.

In what we assumed to be the lobby, a very small, prissy-
looking, gum-chewing young woman was engaged in conversation with a surly, cretinous-looking young man, with a
massive lower lip and thick, matted black hair (a stableboy
type, were this Victorian fiction). We at last were able to
disengage the young woman, who was at last able to find our
reservations—for a week; even then I was not sure that I
could stick it out. And the cretin showed us, reluctantly, to
our rooms.

They were small and dark and cold and dirty. We each had a small fireplace in one corner, with a small, dirty, empty grate; we were told that fires would be built between seven and eight that night. And, naturally, no hot water. In the tiny closet, no rack or nails or any device for hanging up clothes.

We went out for a walk, in what had become a very cold and penetrating rain.

We found the cathedral, which is relatively small and beautifully carved, its façade both tidy and complex (begun in the seventeenth century and finished in the eighteenth, it was badly damaged by an earthquake in 1901. It is the only cathedral in Mexico with an *artesonado* ceiling—which means beams and/or panels with painting and inlay, a Moorish custom). One of the reasons first impelling me to come to San Cristóbal was a sentence uttered by a young historian, specializing in church history: "San Cristóbal has the most beautiful baroque architecture in Mexico." This is quite possibly true, though at that moment, in the rain, it seemed not quite worth it.

We found a pleasant café with an open fire, where we dried off a little. Then we went back to our hotel to change from wet clothes and to try to wash.

In the restaurant across the street, where we went for dinner, we were served the smallest margaritas I had ever seen. "This looks like half a margarita," I said to the waiter.

"That's what it is, a half-margarita."

"Oh."

At the next table some students were talking about Tuxtla Gutiérrez, which was to be our taking-off place for Mexico City. "God, it was so hot," they said. "The heat—"

Looking across at Cynthia, I knew very well that we would be in Tuxtla very soon.

"You could change your flight from Mexico City," she said, intensely. "Get home a couple of days early."

A very attractive prospect, at that moment. Also, I was very drawn to the notion of freedom that Cynthia was conjuring up for me. I have always tended to make travel plans and stick to them, and here she was suggesting that you could change your mind and act on impulse. Be somewhat whimsical. A very seductive idea, all around.

All that night huge trucks thundered past my window, and cars, all sounding their horns. But the next morning was pale and clear, lovely clean air—and in my bathroom there was hot water. I had a very long, marvelously stinging, very hot shower.

"We could get a car to Tuxtla this afternoon," said Cynthia at breakfast. "And then go to a travel agent there and maybe fly out tomorrow."

"But tickets. Hotels."

"We can change all that."

The upshot was that we went to an agent and hired a car to take us to Tuxtla that afternoon, and we reserved hotel rooms there. At the desk of the Hotel España, where we went to announce our departure, we found a great cluster of guests, all gathered around the desk to complain: no heat, no hot water, noise at night.

We spent the morning dutifully exploring San Cristóbal—which must have been named for Bartolomé de Las Casas (1474–1566), a Spanish missionary and historian and one of the few Spaniards ever who, during the Conquest, took up the cause of the Indians, pointing out to the Spanish that the Indians were being most miserably exploited. For a while (1544–1547) he was the bishop of Chiapas, and almost entirely through his efforts the so-called New Laws for the protection of Indians were enacted. Alas, to little avail.

THE DAY was clear but very cold; Cynthia and I took pictures of each other huddled in doorways, wearing many layers of all the wrong clothes.

Aside from the baroque architecture, we had also wanted to see the Na Bolom Center, a museum-library established by the Danish writer-explorer Frans Blom and his wife and colleague, Trudy Blom, who almost single-handedly saved the Lacandón Indians from extinction. But the center was closed.

And the town had still the enclosed, defended quality that had first struck us. There seemed no way out from the maze of streets; we felt entrapped, despite distant and pretty views of outside hills and meadows.

We went to an open market where there were some good woven shawls and blankets—and some beautiful, small dark and staring Indian children. Many wore clothes that seemed just slightly too large, little girls in too-long plaid wool skirts and big sweaters, with long black hair that was not quite combed and large, black, reproachful eyes.

Back at the Hotel España, we saw some of the charm that Mr. Greene felt, in the sunny, flowery courtyard, with its nice tiled fountain and lacy wrought-iron furniture. But it was still very cold and full of complaining tourists.

THE DRIVE to Tuxtla Gutiérrez was mostly beautiful, and we were elated at what felt like an escape from San Cristóbal into almost instant warmth. The mountains had the same abrupt, unexpected sharp shapes that we had seen on the drive from Palenque, and there were lovely low-lying plains in the sunlight, here and there crossed with long cloud shadows. And we went over a high bridge that crossed a most beautiful gorge: the Chiapas River, with its high, white, sculptured cliffs on either side.

Our entrance into the town of Tuxtla Gutiérrez was more than a little daunting, though. Understatedly described by our most reliable guidebook as "not one of the country's most magnificent tourist towns," it looked to Cynthia and to me quite simply and unmitigatedly ugly, incredibly ugly—and nothing later was ever to change that first view. The main street and every other street that we saw, for those hellish days in Tuxtla, was garish, dirty, and noisy. Only the heat was welcome, and we quite soon had too much of that. In no way, really, does Tuxtla look "Mexican"; it could be Fairbanks, Alaska, or Durham, North Carolina.

Here is Graham Greene on Tuxtla: "Tuxtla is not a place for foreigners—the new ugly capital of Chiapas, without attractions. . . . It is like an unnecessary postscript to Chiapas, which should be all wild mountains and old churches and swallowed ruins . . ." (*Lawless Roads,* 194). Indeed.

Our hotel was middle-middle-middle-class commercial, entirely lacking in charm but possessed of a strangely ugly, large swimming pool. Also a coffee shop and a fancy-looking restaurant, near the pool, in an odd pink structure, vaguely "French."

My room, on first sight, was perfectly okay, if unattractive. At the rear of the hotel, the room's windows faced some palm trees, and mountains, and lots of sky.

Feeling efficient, and mobilized, right away Cynthia and I asked at the desk for a travel agency; we were determined to get out of there as soon as possible—to fly to Mexico City and then home (I to D., Cynthia to her Chicago gallery). There was no travel agency, we were told, but with luck we could make it to the airline office that day. This was a

Friday. My reservations out of Mexico City were for the following Wednesday, as were Cynthia's—but we planned to change all that.

We rushed out and along the hideous main street, and indeed we made it to the airline office half an hour before closing time. Where we got this news: There were no planes, absolutely none at all, from Tuxtla to Mexico City until the following Tuesday. However, we were both able to change our flights from Mexico City to Chicago and to San Francisco, respectively, from Wednesday back to Tuesday.

But: Four more days in Tuxtla? We had planned on one, had only come to use Tuxtla as a jumping-off place. Already this seemed an impossibility, more than we could bear. (But what do you do with a fact that you cannot bear? I have more than once wondered.)

"Suppose we rented a car and drove to Oaxaca, and got a plane from there," Cynthia suggested.

We discussed this plan—the mountain ranges involved, the possibility of no planes from Oaxaca either, maybe no hotels—and the fact that I don't drive. And although we were indeed desperate, increasingly desperate, we gave it up.

And so: four more days in Tuxtla.

ONE PROBLEM, making this impossible situation worse, was that I was out of books to read; a part of my all-around poor planning for this trip was a failure to bring along more good, long books. And Cynthia's assortment was odd: *Gravity's Rainbow* (I had read this once before under better—in fact under very good—circumstances and found it very hard going indeed; it would have been impossible to read Pynchon in Tuxtla). And Paul Bowles's *The Sheltering Sky*. I had read this before, too, and very much liked it. And so I reread Paul Bowles—and now, in my remembered view of myself in Tuxtla, I am lying on that bed, in that room, reading about Americans getting lost in a foreign desert, about illness, disintegration, death—while the glass panes on my window rattle fiercely, in a hot (desert) wind, and outside the palm fronds shake. And black clouds gather around the mountain, covering its village.

I CALLED D. collect, who kindly said that time dragged for him, without me. I thanked him, and sympathized, but I really thought: You don't know the first thing about dragging time until you've put in time in Tuxtla Gutiérrez.

I told D. that I would be home a day earlier, and he was very pleased, he said.

CYNTHIA GOT sick but recovered; I got well, and we went off to the zoo, an extremely strange, large wooded area where it is almost impossible to see any of the animals, although it is supposed to contain wonderful specimens of wildlife from all over Chiapas. But the animals all managed to obscure themselves in the underbrush, although occasionally a snout or a spot protruded. In my snapshots of the Tuxtla zoo, what you see are great heaps of dead leaves, in corners, or up against fences.

An interesting fact, we thought, was that all the zoo attendants were exceptionally good-looking young women.

As we were leaving we were accosted by a group of children, a couple of girls and a little boy, who wanted to try out their English.

"Where are you from? Do you much like Mexico? Do you stay much time in Tuxtla Gutiérrez?"

We talked for a while, telling them, I am sure, somewhat more than they wanted to know, and then parted with high ceremoniousness all around. And then, as we walked on our way, from behind us we heard, amid bursts of giggles, "I love you! Ladies, I love you!"

W E SWAM and lay beside the pool in the sun, activities that I normally enjoy a great deal, but Cynthia was so much younger (and thinner, and blonder) than I am that I found it slightly depressing.

We walked down to the *zócalo*, looking for a bookstore, for anything whatsoever to read. The *zócalo* was an exceptionally ugly stretch of more-or-less unrelieved concrete, and we found not a single bookstore.

We did find, though, a man selling coconut milk.

"It's perfectly okay to drink," said Cynthia.

"Are you sure?"

"Oh yes, I drank it all the time in Guatemala."

We bought some and drank it, and the taste was absolutely delicious—and it made us both very sick by that night, a night that was surely the nadir of our trip.

T HE NEXT day I had a pedicure, something I had never in my life done before, but there it was, advertised by signs in the lobby: "Professional Beauty, Permanent Waves, Manicures, Pedicures, Hair Dying." An available killer of time. It took an hour and cost four dollars, and my feet looked unaccustomedly great, but the process hurt a lot.

"You are too sensitive," the manicurist said—something that I had heard before, especially from my dentist.

"ONE PROBLEM about Tuxtla is that you can get fogged in there." This single sentence, from the travel agent in San Cristóbal, returned to my waking consciousness, in fact it very likely woke me up, about five in the morning of the day on which we were at last to leave. A San Franciscan, I am sensitive to talk of fog. I believe in fog.

The weather looked fairly clear, though, what I could see of it—but I was scared, anxiety-prone.

At breakfast, the waiter whom I had always most disliked—I disliked his dyed and blow-dried hair, his small stupid eyes—was worse than usual. After several mistakes in our orders, which were not complex, and ensuing arguments (he was never wrong, a further source of irritation), Cynthia said, "Do you know? I almost hit that waiter? Can you imagine? I've never hit anyone, not even a husband, much less a waiter."

"He's pretty irritating."

"Do you think there's some sort of local inbreeding that makes them so awful?"

We decided probably not. They simply hated gringos, for which we could not blame them.

WE HAD ordered a cab for far too early, of course, and of course it came precisely on time.

The drive out to the airport seemed endless, and it seemed to us both that we were driving right into fog. "How marvelous of Tuxtla to build its airport on the one foggy spot for miles," we bitterly remarked.

We were an hour and a half early, and we went to sit in a cafeteria, where we watched the shifting clouds with extreme apprehension. I was thinking, and I am sure that Cynthia was too, Just what will we do if this flight is cancelled? Exactly what?

There were to be two flights to Mexico City that morning, ours at 10:30, another at 1:00. And at around 10:00 a large plane duly appeared from the cloudy sky—surely ours. We all began to move toward the door, with all our luggage. To form a line. We stood there, and stood, and stood—while out on the field, beside the plane, official-looking people ran back and forth, back and forth. "That looks like an engineer's outfit, is that a good sign?" Cynthia desperately asked.

An announcement: some small malfunction, to be fixed very soon.

More time passed, quite a lot of time, and another announcement came: A part was needed from Mexico City. It would arrive at any moment.

By this time Cynthia and I hardly dared look at each other, much less speak.

But another plane did arrive, and men who looked to be workmen were seen to effect some sort of transfer between the planes. However, this second plane was obviously destined for the 1:00 flight (it was now about 12:30; we had been out at the airport for about four hours). Passengers were lined up, waiting for that plane, even as we had been. But they, at last, were allowed to board their plane, and it seemed (to us) that they took an unconscionably long time to do so.

They took off.

Perhaps another hour passed. Perhaps fortunately, it is very hard to remember any thoughts from that hour. And then we were allowed to board our plane. To leave Tuxtla Gutiérrez. For good.

WE WOULD arrive in Mexico City at 4:00. Cynthia's Chicago plane would leave at 5:00, mine for San Francisco not until 8:30. I toyed with plans: Sitting in the airport for all that time seemed onerous; on the other hand, I lacked the stamina, I felt, for a solitary trek into Mexico City, for museums, whatever, and then a trip back out to the airport. What I wanted most in the world, I thought, was a swim—and then I thought, why not? An airport motel with a pool? One of the few virtues, I guess the only virtue, of our stay in Tuxtla was that it had been extremely cheap, I had spent almost no money, and so an afternoon motel seemed a reasonable indulgence.

In the Mexico City airport, after saying goodbye to Cynthia, I found that there was a hotel next to the airport, the Fiesta Americana, that indeed had a pool, they said. And almost immediately I found a bellboy from that hotel, who would meet me at the front desk with my bags, he said.

Luggageless, I walked up the designated stairs, across a ramp, and into a mammoth commercial-looking lobby, and I registered at the desk. But no bags came.

Because of the press of time, and generalized anxiety engendered by that whole trip, and particularly its last (Tuxtla) chapter, I was more than usually impatient. And by the time they did come, after twenty minutes or so, I was considerably annoyed, and frayed.

My room was perfectly okay, though, with what looked to be a more-than-adequate shower. The pool was up on the twelfth floor, I was told.

The "pool" turned out to be in a room called the Skylight Bar, and what they meant by pool was a long, upraised rubber tank. From an outside deck, surrounding the room, one could see the fumes and strange towers of Mexico City; I chose the tank over the deck, and I swam up and down, like a very oversized white fish, while in the nightclub part of the room a singer practiced with the mike (a black North American, very thin and handsome, with a marvelous voice). I ordered a club sandwich and a beer, which I took at poolside, so to speak.

I had forgotten to bring a towel up with me but congratulated myself that I had not forgotten anything more crucial, like the key—what with general and particular stresses, all around.

But: I could not get the key to open the door. I am not very good with keys and often have trouble with strange ones, and so I gave it some time and what patience I could summon, but with no luck, no budge of the lock. And so I went looking for a bellboy, or any possibly helpful person—in my wet cold suit, barely covered by a cotton shirt.

I found a bellboy, and he was also unable to open my door.

He called the housekeeper, who had the same problem. She assured me that there would be no charge for my room.

An hour later a locksmith got the door open. I took a very quick hot shower, dressed, and hurried out. At the desk I was told that the housekeeper had said nothing about my problem, nor any free room. But I did not dare take more time to argue; the way things were going, I thought, I did not dare risk some foul-up with my ticket—which, after all, I had changed in Tuxtla Gutiérrez.

At the airline counter I found that I was indeed on the manifest, and the only hitch in leaving was that I was sent to Gate B, instead of C, from which the plane departed.

In the lounge where (it now seemed very long ago, thirteen days) I had written that long letter to D., full of premature longing, I now had a farewell margarita.

And I got on my plane, barely able to believe what I was doing.

The news on the plane was that Ortega had lost the election in Nicaragua. I learned this from a very thin, in fact sick-looking young man (he explained: a week with no sleep), a lawyer who had been down there inspecting the election. "This is a great victory for George Bush," he said, very bitterly. "For the C.I.A."

A young North American woman joined us. In a serape top, much silver jewelry, she looked as though she had been living down there forever. And she almost had: She was just leaving Oaxaca after a fifteen-year residence there, she said. It just wasn't great anymore, she was sick all the time and had just found out that floods drained sewage into the water system. "It's all really fucked," she said. "It's over in Mexico."

The young lawyer agreed with her.

Which I have to admit is more or less how I myself felt, at that time. I felt that Mexico had become, or at least was becoming, unbearable. That tourists were being forced down the throats of Mexicans because that poor country so desperately needs the tourist industry, creating an impossible circle of need and resentment.

GIVEN THE vicissitudes of that trip, it is only reasonable and to be expected that D. and I should fail to find each other at the airport, although he was there, and I was there, and we looked for each other, albeit at considerably divergent hours: He had been misinformed by the airline.

I finally gave up and took a taxi to my house, where he (finally) called and eventually arrived—by which time I was much too tired to tell him much about my trip, which at that moment was probably just as well.

CHAPTER
NINE

GUADALAJARA

NE STRONG reason for going to Guadalajara was the contradictory extremes of various stated reactions to that city: It's really beautiful, don't miss it. Crowded and filthy, another Mexico City. Very interesting colonial architecture. The greatest shopping in Mexico, don't miss the market. Guadalajara is utterly ruined, forget it.

I was also, naturally, drawn by the fact that it is an easy trip from San Francisco, a simple three-hour flight, with no changing in Mexico City.

The final and compelling factor was that I was able to talk my son and a friend of his into coming along. Peter, a sculptor-painter, and Phil, an architect. (Impossible to describe a person one likes as much as I do Peter—let me simply say that he is smart, funny, kind; and that Phil is extremely nice, too.) Not having been to Mexico before, their plans were somewhat ambitious, though; they saw Guadalajara as a good central location from which to travel to Guanajuato, Pátzcuaro, San Miguel, Morelia—God knows where. The very contemplation of so many places made me tired, but I agreed, on condition that they would make all the travel arrangements. I would go along with anything, I rashly said.

The trip down, as I had hoped, was easy and pleasant. A bright clear day, smooth flight. Not having seen this terrain before, Peter and Phil were much taken with the views of giant bare mountain ranges, and the Sea of Cortés, down below us.

The other passengers seemed pleasant. Many of them were Mexican-Americans, going back home for a visit (there is a large colony of Mexicans from Guadalajara in San Francisco, as well as in Los Angeles). One woman was especially striking in that she had bright white hair, tossed in what used to be called a poodle cut, and she carried in her arms a matching white poodle that on closer inspection turned out to be a doll. Her husband, a small, trim, gray-haired man, wore a much-decorated army uniform—either from the Spanish-American War or from a marching band; it was hard to tell in his confusion of braids and medals. There were also fat grand-mothers and shrieking children, and pretty young girls with their new-looking husbands, all off to Mexico for Easter, a more important holiday in Mexico than even Christmas is.

And, having left San Francisco in characteristic April cold and fog, we arrived in a warm and flowery climate—not quite the tropics, not Zihuatanejo, but very nice. As we drove from the airport into the city, purple jacaranda was everywhere in delicate bloom.

In the matter of the hotel, too, Peter had done very well: a small and cheerfully run, tidy place, and perfectly located: about two blocks from the *zócalo*. In fact, as the days went by, I came to feel that we inhabited a very small but peaceful and beautiful area of what is basically a large and ugly city; if one went to Guadalajara and never left that island, where we were, the *zócalo* and its adjoining open city spaces, one would imagine an almost enchanted city. But that is not what we did.

Our first view of the *zócalo* was a considerable delight: a long square where fountains played and leisurely people strolled about with dogs and children, and high-held balloons. An immediate impression of Guadalajara is one of relative prosperity; it seems to be a city where people are mostly employed, you do not see anything like the numbers of desperately poor, homeless beggars that you see in Mexico City—or in San Francisco, or in New York.

At one end of that long, heterogeneous space is the grandly columned Degollado Theater; at the other the cathedral, an exuberantly confused structure, with almost-twin spires and a couple of mismatched domes, all very richly tiled in gold.

The theater advertised the Ballet Folklorica—and so (why not? there we were) we bought tickets for the following day, a Sunday, for 10:00 A.M.—surely the oddest hour at which I had ever gone to the theater, but then again, why not?

Inside the cathedral, our next destination, there was further confusion: The statues were all draped with thick covering, like summer furniture, for Lent, but there were flowers everywhere, mostly huge sprays of white gladioli. And people stood before the statues and prayed to them as fervently as though the plaster saints and holy figures were visible, uncovered. (Perhaps they knew them by heart, so to speak?) I watched a very pretty, dark, rather shabby young woman who approached the large altar on her knees, her expression at once shy and abashed, proud and very fervent.

THE MARKET, said to be the largest in the world, is indeed immense: four stories high, all jammed with stalls selling everything. They must attain a certain local reputation, those stalls, I thought; a really knowledgeable shopper would know that the leather belts in the third stall to the left of the third-floor stairs were by far the best. But with no such informational equipment we simply walked around, somewhat dazed. Peter and Phil, less accustomed than I to this Mexican plethora of bargains, were more tempted, here and there;

also, less frequent travelers, and very generous men, they both had lists—of friends and cousins, coworkers and extended family members. I only wanted some very beautiful and very cheap opal rings to replace the ones that I used to buy on the beach at Zihuatanejo; they cost about ten dollars and are indeed very lovely, at first, but they dull and also tend to fall out of their flimsy settings. I found my new rings fairly easily (it is interesting, the amount of time that one can spend choosing between two ten-dollar rings), and I bought a gray lizard belt for D., who, I imagined, probably would not like it.

Next to the market and very much a part of it was a sort of terraced amphitheater, where people sat and talked and told stories and mostly compared their purchases. We sat down next to some cages of wonderful white birds, whose tails were most elegantly fanned out (what a nifty present for my cats, I thought). We sat there for quite a while, admiring the birds and eavesdropping on knowledgeable mercantile discussions, along with gossip of marriages and births, of sales and deaths.

THE ROOMS in our hotel were ugly but very quiet and practical: Everything worked. Registering there, I had no impulse to use my newly acquired room-changing skill. And the public rooms downstairs were also fairly charmless but practical.

AT BREAKFAST the waiters would always, if at all possible, dump all the Americans into a single room, and so I often found myself in the company of my compatriots: middle-aged couples with sulky, restless, adolescent children, spoiled by travel; serious elderly travelers, with lots of guidebooks. And young singles, very young girls and boys who seemed to be part of some tour. Also, in this particular hotel, there was an apparently resident North American drunk, who chain-smoked and clipped his nails at the table, never seeming to eat; he was treated with gentle joviality by all the waiters, they took good care of him.

Also (interesting to know why this particular couple was seated among the gringos) a very short dark man (his hair quite possibly dyed), middle-aged or older, with an extremely young hooker-type girl, with very long curled hair and very very high thin heels. She was very serious with him, whereas he was jokey, cajoling—as though in the night he had made serious promises that she wanted to discuss, and he was saying, "Come on, you know I didn't really mean that."

THE AUDIENCE at the Ballet Folklorica at ten on Sunday morning consisted mostly of fairly dressed-up North Americans, a great many of whom seemed to know each other. The colony.

There were many dances, one for each region of Mexico, but they all bore strong similarities to each other; they were, in fact, far too much what one would have expected them to be—long skirts and tight long-sleeved tops, with very high heels. Plain suits and white shirts for the men. The women did a great deal of stamping about and skirt swinging. (Peter: "Skirt swinging seems to be a big outlet for women down here.") The men did various tricky things with their hats, and they stamped quite a lot too.

For sheer dullness, the Veracruz section was most remarkable; the phrase "—nights in Veracruz!" was repeated eight or ten times. In another dance, I believe from Jalisco, waiter-dancers held glasses of water on their hats, some of which spilled, to everyone's great amusement. In still another dance, knots were tied and then untied with the dancers' feet.

BREATHING DEEPLY, after so much "performance," we went out to a park, the Parque Agua Azul, and there found a most wonderful variety of trees, eucalyptus and elms, much lovely jacaranda in flower—all those tall trees waving there above the grass where somnolent couples lay about in various states of disarranged clothing, in various degrees of embrace. As lively children and small yapping dogs ran about all over.

Next to the park is the Archaeology Museum, very small and very good: full of small pre-Columbian figures, from Colima. Crude and vigorous.

ALTHOUGH I am in many ways an experienced traveler, I am still very bad at packing. I have improved somewhat. I now deal with the anxiety that packing always engenders by giving it a very long time, say, a full afternoon. Still, I make serious mistakes, my tendency being to omit at least one crucial thing. In the interests of anxiety-reduction I repeat to myself that I can buy whatever it is that I have forgotten, probably. Which is all very well if I am going to New York and have left a favorite lipstick in San Francisco. However, the crucial thing that I neglected to bring to Guadalajara was the vial of tranquilizers that I occasionally take for sleep, and perhaps as a consequence of that lapse, I slept very badly there.

I asked at the desk for some sleeping pills, and the pleasant young woman responded warmly, a fellow insomniac, probably; she gave me a brand name and described the pharmacy two blocks away at which these pills would be available.

They came in a large black box, these wonder pills, and the bottle itself was black and scary-looking, as the description was scary: "For calming tremors that affect the brain." Finally I did not dare take one, and I asked about my own American brand (which is probably no good for me either, but at least it does not mention tremors affecting the brain in its advertisements).

Ah, for that I would need a prescription, I was told.

After another night of no sleep at all, although it seemed quite self-indulgent (I was not sick), I called a doctor—or rather the hotel called the doctor for me; he seemed more or less part of their staff, and he arrived in an hour or so at my door, a fat young man with thinning hair, all dripping with sweat. He took my blood pressure, which is variously described as "borderline high" and "labile" and talked a great deal about what to say to my own doctor, back in San Francisco; my feeling was that he was anxious to impress this distant doctor. But he gave me the requisite prescription, and I went out and got the pills for very little money, in a government-run pharmacy. And I recovered from my sleeplessness in the cool hotel pool, which was very pleasant. It even had a sort of ersatz-Barragán broken arch, as decoration, across one end.

MANY YEARS ago, when I first went to Mexico, all sorts of prescription drugs were available over the counter, and in the relatively innocent, predrug days of the fifties, friends would ask for presents of "diet pills." In fact, the new ruling about prescriptions came only in 1989, I was told.

AFTER MAKING various inquiries, Peter and Phil (who were still in charge, as far as I was concerned) decided that a trip to Guanajuato or San Miguel was simply too far and that we would only go to Lake Pátzcuaro, for the day. They found a driver, a handsome young man named Carlos, who said, Oh yes, Pátzcuaro. Two or three hours, Very easy.

It was almost too easily arranged, but we all looked forward to this trip.

But early the next morning I had a call from Carlos (Why me? I am not sure). Very elaborately, and endlessly, he told me that there were troubles with his car, and his wife was not well, and also there was fighting in Michoacán because of the last election. And so on.

"Carlos, are you trying to say that you can't drive us today?"

"I do not trust my car, and then since the last election, the forces of the PRI—"

I finally got him off the phone and went downstairs to break this news to Peter and Phil, at breakfast. Disappointed but quite undaunted, they went out to the street to talk to one of the cab drivers, Maximilian, a loquacious fellow who had driven us home from a restaurant the night before, treating us as he did so to a lecture on Cárdenas: "He has some very good ideas, big plans, but you must remember that his father had many, many Communist friends." (Why do so many of us try to take a country's political pulse from its cab drivers? This is really silly, when you come to think of it; they are quite as apt to be as full of baloney and misinformation as we ourselves are. It is rather like the old myth about truck drivers and restaurants, I think.)

But the deal was struck. It would take at least three-and-a-half hours to drive to Pátzcuaro, said Maximilian (so much for Carlos, the ignorant optimist). We were to start the following morning at nine.

And so we did. The three of us piled (Peter and Phil are both tall) into a smallish, creaking cab—all of us, I assume, with some unexpressed misgivings. Max, short and round and red-faced, that day wearing a bright red shirt, was full of expostulations: Ah, Dios! Holy Mother! Damn to hell!—and jokes, which I am happily unable to remember. It even occurred to me that he might be drunk, a possibility that I quickly dismissed as simply too horrible, and I decided that he was just nervous, as we were.

The road seemed to match our vehicle. Full of potholes, it bounced and shook us along, exacerbating our creaks and rattles. And since the road was narrow, we were almost always stuck in a very long line behind a couple of huge heavy trucks.

It takes a good four-and-a-half hours to get anywhere near Pátzcuaro.

A CURIOUS travelers' impulse that I have observed in both myself and in others is that which leads one to seek out places where you have been before, even if nothing very good or even significant happened to you there. So it was with me in Pátzcuaro: I walked all over the small and unattractive lakeside town where years before (before we even went to Zihuatanejo) I had lunched with R., looking for a restaurant that we had not even especially liked and of which my strongest memory was a dog being very sick in the road outside.

We had also been disappointed, I now remembered, because the fabled fishermen with their butterfly nets were nowhere to be seen, then as now; what we saw was the central island, Janitzio Island, with its giant sculpture of Father Morelos—one of the major heros in the first fight for independence from Spain.

The town itself, Pátzcuaro, is small, and that day was crowded with a Lenten festival. We arranged to meet Max later, and we set out to walk about—and found some quite wonderful buildings, notably a church with murals by Juan O'Gorman—and a tourist bureau and craft center.

But possibly our favorites were the long exhibits of bread, table after table of the most wonderfully shaped loaves, of all sizes and colors, some ornately decorated with wreathes and flowers, fish and birds. Philip bought a sack of bread, which I thought rather greedy at the time (we had had some very good whitefish from the lake for lunch) but for which later on we were all most grateful.

Near Pátzcuaro is a village exotically called Tzintzuntzán, which means "the place of the hummingbirds" and which was the ancient capital of the Tarascans—and where these days there are interesting ruins, some circular, with the characteristic, very high, very narrow steps, and all affording the prettiest views yet of Lake Pátzcuaro.

THE DRIVE home took something over five hours and was, of course, a repetition: the same potholes, the same endless waits behind diesel-spewing trucks.

We gratefully ate all of Philip's bread.

When we got home, at last, only the bar was open—where, again with gratitude, we had a beer.

W E WENT out to Tlaquepaque, which was formerly (around the end of the last century) a prized vacation spot for Guadalajarans; it has not been so since the Revolution and the almost simultaneous advent of the motorcar.

One can see former prettiness in the sequence of squares, the nice trees—but today the plethora of pure junk, shop after shop of horrors, is overwhelming. Many of the stores are indeed, as Kate Simon put it, "tourist traps, museums of ineptitude and dynamic bad taste." (*Mexico: Places and Pleasures, 271*)

At lunch, out on a terrace (the several restaurants are identical), we were befriended by a very scruffy, exceptionally polite dog, who seemed grateful for some chicken *mole*. (It is not my impression that domestic animals are much looked after in Mexico, and indeed how could they be, in a near-starvation population?)

Peter and Phil continued their well-intentioned search for presents, hoping always for the miracle of a Good Thing—among all that garbage.

A ND WE went out to another small town, Tapalpa, supposedly a marvelous center of crafts (various guidebooks say so, even the good ones), where we found booth after booth (again) of unrelieved junk, junk, junk.

One display, though, was great: a cluster of baskets of herbs, each with miraculous medicinal properties. A sign above each basket proclaimed the name of the ailment to be cured: Nerves, Muscular Pain, Headaches, Diabetes, Lack of

Dreams, Blood Circulation, Problems of Sexuality, Cancer. Well, surely that just about covers things? I have been wondering though, about the herb for lack of dreams; it could have been something exciting.

ALTHOUGH WE had become fond of the series of squares behind the Degollado Theater, known as the Plaza Tapatía (people from Guadalajara are called *tapatíos,* from an Indian phrase that means "three times as worthy," a proud and boastful nickname), and we had admired the imposing façade of the building known as the Orphanage, the Hospicio Cabañas, it was not until almost our last day in Guadalajara that we managed to get there at a time when the place was open (strange, unpublicized hours of opening and closing can be a problem in Mexico). No longer an orphanage, it is now a cultural center, housing some of Orozco's most magnificent murals—a ceiling of murals, in fact, that is quite overwhelming: four gigantic male figures, supposedly representing Earth, Wind, Water, and Fire. Orozco always refused to elaborate further.

Also magnificent are the stone fireplaces, huge and very plain; one imagines pigs on spits, at the very least.

It is hard indeed to imagine orphans in this place. How awestruck they must have been, poor mites.

WE WATCHED a mime troop's lively display in the main square, near the largest fountain. Signs proclaimed this as a socialist group, presumably for Cárdenas, but it was a little hard to find the political message in the slapstick of courtship (as in the Folklorico, courtship was the major theme). A very pretty girl was chosen from the audience (I am quite sure, not at random), and her marriage was arranged by the painted mime—to a very ordinary, not-handsome husband. A priest was found, behind whom was a crucified Jesus figure (anticlericalism is socialism?) A few clothes were removed, not many—to violent audience giggles. The groom, I guess in a state of amorous confusion, then kissed the mime: more giggles and sounds of shock. It was all very good-natured and fairly skillful; still, it was hard to find the socialist voice.

INSIDE THE cathedral, on Maundy Thursday (this is the day on which you are supposed to go to seven churches), there was a complicated ceremony known as the Blessing of the Infirm: people on crutches, in wheelchairs, and one poor very sick young man (maybe AIDS) on a gurney. All these sad people were laboriously wheeled up to the altar, among throngs of worshipers and a singularly inept and ubiquitous TV crew, who managed to be more present than any other element, noisier and more in the way. In the back, where we three were standing, babies screamed and screeched from their mothers' arms, but in the general confusion no one turned to look (in Mexico, crying babies are much more taken for granted than they tend to be up here).

And somehow, in all that confusion, the plight of the ill and the maimed became lessened, if not lost. One can only hope that somehow they were helped.

ON GOOD Friday, our last day in Guadalajara, there was a marvelous small concert in the square next to the church: A group of boys, maybe about twenty years old, played two guitars, a tiny banjo, a drum, and two reed pipes. These instruments were passed about among the players, and the effect was of strong communality, a literally joint endeavor. And the music was wild; never have I heard such a dionysian "Sleepers Wake"—in that intense late-afternoon heat, in the unsheltering semishade of several flowering jacaranda trees.

WHY, ON our last night in Guadalajara, did we choose to go to a Japanese restaurant, highly touted in all the tourist magazines? I am not sure, unless we were prompted by the sort of longing for another cuisine that can afflict one almost anywhere (in Italy, I remember once longing for Chinese food, San Francisco style—and there is always the great American craving for a hamburger). In any case, we did go to the Japanese restaurant, which was interestingly Japanese country-inn style, in design—and wondrously clean and tidy, in fact I would have to describe cleanliness as its greatest virtue. The food was poor and served with incredible slowness by Mexican girls who seemed imperfectly instructed; ours dished it out kernel of rice by kernel, or almost. But the crowds of Japanese tourists who continued to show up there, in throngs, seemed quite pleased with everything, happy to be there, temporarily dissociated from Mexico.

EARLY ON in our stay in Guadalajara, we came upon, or rather climbed up some stairs to, a restaurant on the *zócalo,* called Sandy's. It was a very pleasant place, from which we looked down through a filagree of pale green leaves to the street and the square below, and across to the curious cathedral domes. They served good iced coffee and a variety of good fresh fruit juices; we often repaired to Sandy's for refreshment—and it was there that in a leisurely, unstructured way we discussed our trip. Or rather, I mostly listened to Peter and Phil, the first-time travelers.

And here, somewhat at random, are a few of their observations (limited, of course, to Guadalajara):

It's very European. People stroll as a daily activity, like shopping (as they do in Paris).

The churches are public places, always in use, and with many uses, including socializing.

There are fewer street people than in San Francisco, or New York.

There are almost no recognizable gay people.

There is less display of wealth by middle-class people than in the States (or perhaps the middle class is less wealthy?) There are impressive homes behind closed doors, and the privacy of the inner courtyard.

Tremendous display of wealth, on the other hand, by churches.

B UT WHAT do you really mean, I asked them, when you say that something looks Mexican?

Very bright colors, put together in ways you would not expect: turquoise and orange and yellow and red, in big stripes.

Very large architectural decorations. Less detail and more enlargement. An overall effect of roughness. And the large details stand out in contrast to plain surfaces.

O CTAVIO PAZ writes about contrasts in Mexico, Peter reminded me. Polarities. Festive and somber. Shadow and light. And, when you get down to it, life and death.

I WANT very much to go back to Guadalajara.

CHAPTER
TEN

MEXICO CITY,
AND
FRIDA KAHLO

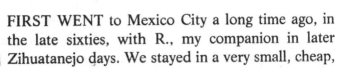

FIRST WENT to Mexico City a long time ago, in the late sixties, with R., my companion in later Zihuatanejo days. We stayed in a very small, cheap, and pretty colonial hotel, not far off the Reforma, near the Zona Rosa. (The size of the closet in that hotel was the only problem: unused to travel, at that time, and unaware of the concept of traveling light, we brought along almost all our summer clothes.)

We walked everywhere, and we had on the whole a splendid time. Mostly we walked along the Reforma, up to the *zócalo*, the Cathedral and Alameda Park, and then all the way down to Chapultepec Park.

We looked at a new hotel, just then under construction, near Chapultepec—the Camino Real, designed by a student of Luis Barragán, the great Mexican architect. It looked very glamorous, that hotel, and not at all the sort of place where we would ever stay.

The fumes in Mexico City in those days were bad but not intolerable (R., with more sensitive eyes, minded more than I did). The same could be said of the general level of noise. It certainly was, even then, a vastly overpopulated, dirty, and polluted city, but we were more aware of a fascinating and often beautiful variety of architecture (Moorish-colonial to

203

Barragán-modern), of elegant city spaces (Alameda Park, Chapultepec), and of the broad and elegant Reforma itself, very like a Spanish boulevard in Madrid or Barcelona. We found good restaurants and interesting shops.

And museums: It was there, on that trip, that I saw my first Frida Kahlo.

"Who is Frida Kahlo? I never heard of her."

"She was married to Diego Rivera," R. told me.

"Actually, I like her painting better than his."

That conversation took place in the Museum of Modern Art, in Chapultepec. We were standing before her large and magnificent *The Two Fridas.* What is perhaps most striking, what struck me most then and continues to do so, is the contrast between the serenity of the posture and expressions of the same dark and tragically beautiful woman, seen twice— and the fact of the blood that is dripping onto the lap of one woman, from a severed artery. It would be inaccurate to say that I thought with great frequency of that incident and of the painting in the months and years after that, for I did not; still, there it was, recalled intact.

R. AND I continued for several days to walk about and to enjoy the city. We often took cabs as well, which were cheap and plentiful, but for some reason we took an interminable bus trip (with a janitor from the University of Minnesota) down to the University City—which we both found disappointing: The fabled mosaics were gaudy rather than beautiful, everything jarred. Also (this was in 1967), preparations were already underway for the 1968 Olympics— a summer of such disaster for Mexico City and the nation: months of increasingly bloody confrontations between two opposing coalitions (students and workers; the army and police) ending with the Tlatelolco Massacre on October 2, in which students were indiscriminately gunned down, along with their parents, and children.

There were no hints of such horrors, obviously, but there was great disorder and a general sense that already the whole thing was a great mistake.

WE WENT from the university to San Angel, to a restoratively beautiful and excellent lunch at the San Angel Inn. We did not go to the Diego and Frida museums, which are almost next door to the Inn—not knowing they were there. And we spent time wandering around Coyoacán— again, not going to Frida's blue house, not having heard of it.

One night we went to an uptown bar for a drink, uptown meaning far up the Reforma, near the *zócalo*. We found a pleasant, if too New York–looking place, a more or less anonymously expensive bar—but for my vertiginous taste much too high up, with far too long a downward view. And, for no particular reason, I further complained, "I'd hate to be here in an earthquake."

This is simply something that San Franciscans say, and I suppose we always will, until all of us are buried. Still, R. chose to find it an exceptionally silly remark.

"Why do you say that? It's a brand-new building, un-doubtedly earthquake-proof," he told me. (As I write this it occurs to me that I might have frightened him: Having lived through the Long Beach earthquake, in 1920-something, R. feared earthquakes even more than most of us do.)

And, a week or so later, beside the pool of a horrible hotel in Acapulco, we read that indeed there had been a "minor" earthquake and that the very hotel in which we had had our drink had suffered considerable damage.

O UR STAY in Mexico City, that time, was to end with the delivery of a rented car, a VW, in which we would then drive up to San Miguel, to Querétaro, Morelia, et cetera, finally dropping off the car in Acapulco and flying home.

The car arrived on schedule; we said goodbye to our nice hotel and pulled out. R. had mapped our exit quite carefully, avoiding the worst, most congested parts of Mexico City; his cautious route even included a stop at a camera store. (I should have said: R. is an exceptionally skillful driver and a person of generally high mechanical skills.) Coming out of that store with fresh film, he got into the car and prepared to back out of the slot in which he had parked. But nothing worked, the car would not back out. After many minutes of labor, of swearing, imprecations, R. got out and pushed the car backwards (I got out too, of course) and out into the street. We then started off again, and all the way up to San Miguel we had, with small variants, the following conversation:

R: "This does not make sense. There is no way to get this car into reverse."

A: "They must have given us a VW with no reverse. Let's take it back and complain."

R: "I'm very mechanically oriented. If anyone could get it into reverse, I could."

A: "It must be missing something."

R: "What I don't understand is how those guys who brought it over maneuvered it around the hotel. I could swear they had to back it up."

All through that otherwise quite beautiful and reasonably carefree trip, R. would park that defective car with a careful eye to getting out without going into reverse, which we could not do. He made fine and very complicated calculations that sometimes went awry, so that he was forced (again) to get out and push the car along, backwards, himself (as I stood by: too humiliating to let me push it too, he felt)—to the great delight of the cluster of Mexicans who had gathered to watch. So funny, an oversized, well-dressed, and prosperous-looking American, a big healthy gringo so utterly defeated by a shabby little car, what a good joke.

In Morelia we accidentally ran into (in our hotel dining room) a San Francisco architect who was traveling with his fifteen-year-old son—and yes, you guessed it: The son was able to instruct R. in the mysteries of getting old VWs into reverse gear—and I should point out that on the whole R. took this rather well, quite sportingly.

AFTER THAT trip we did not go to Mexico again at all for several years, and then we went to Vallarta, twice, and then we began our long habit of January visits to Zihuatanejo.

During those years Mexico City was for us a place of airport traumas: a scene of lost luggage, of endlessly delayed planes, bad food, and too many bad margaritas. Of extreme dirt and impossible noise and impenetrable loudspoken announcements. It was indeed an encounter with hell, one that we always dreaded.

As further proof of how I felt about Zihuatanejo, I remember saying one morning to R., after an especially horrendous trip the day before, terrible hours in the Mexico City airport, "You know, I'd even go through all of yesterday again for this—" as I gestured through palms and bougainvillea, out to the lovely sea.

NOTHING THAT we heard or read of Mexico City in those days was encouraging. Between 1986 and 1989 the ozone levels tripled, we read; 90 percent of all air samples registered well above World Health Organization standards, many of them 60 percent higher. (By now, of course, it may well be much worse.)

One year, as R. and I flew out and over the city on New Year's Eve, en route to Zihuatanejo, we became aware of an overwhelmingly noxious smell, and below us the whole city seemed enveloped in a thick and yellowish smoke, like that of hell. We later found that for the holiday celebration rubber tires were being burned all over the city.

We read that about 28 million Mexicans lack drinking water and 51 percent have no sewage facilities.

Twelve thousand tons of pollutants are spewed out into the atmosphere from automobiles and industry, *every day*.

WHEN I thought of a return trip to Mexico City, with some friends who had never been there before, I remembered the Camino Real, which would be as far out of the fumes and the general turmoil as one could get, I thought—with advertisements featuring three swimming pools.

And this trip's true object, twenty years after my first contact with her, was Frida Kahlo: I wanted to make a pilgrimage to her house, and I had talked two friends into coming with me—Gloria, a writer, and Mary, an art critic.

ALL OF this more or less began in the spring of eighty-seven, when there was an extraordinary exhibit of Kahlo's work at the Galería de la Raza, in San Francisco. So many painters' work is weakened by its mass presentation in a show, but this was not so with Kahlo's work: The overall effect was cumulative, brilliantly powerful, almost overwhelming. Her sheer painterly skill is often overlooked in violent reactions, one way or another, to her subject matter, but only consummate skill could have produced such meticulous images of pain, and love, and loneliness.

I began to sense then, in San Francisco, a sort of ground swell of interest in both her work and in her life—and the two are inextricable. Kahlo painted what she felt as the central facts of her life: her badly maimed but still beautiful body, and her violent love for Diego. In fact, these days Frida has become a heroine of several groups; she is a heroine as an artist; as a Third World woman; and also as a handicapped woman. And then there is still another group popularly referred to as "women who love too much," the "too much" referring especially to men perceived as bad, as unfaithful and not loving enough in return.

I began to read all I could about Frida Kahlo.

The accident that maimed her occurred when she was eighteen: A streetcar rammed into the trolley in which she was riding, and her spine was broken in seventeen places—it is astonishing that she should have survived. Her pelvis was penetrated by a shaft of metal (a "rape" of which Frida made much), her reproductive organs were gravely injured.

Considerable controversy continues over the precise facts about her injuries. Medical records are lost, or missing. It is now impossible to determine whether she actually did, as she claimed, have seventeen corrective operations; Frida did tend to exaggerate, to mythologize herself, but even a dozen such operations would be quite a lot. It is also uncertain whether she could or could not bear children, or whether she really wanted to. Certainly she was pregnant a number of times and suffered both therapeutic abortions and miscarriages. It would seem to me that she was extremely ambivalent, to say the least, about having children.

She was not ambivalent about Diego; she adored him, she loved him too much.

I N THE course, then, of reading about Frida, of looking at what paintings I could (even in reproduction they are, to me, both intensely beautiful and powerfully moving), and of talking to a few Kahlo scholars, one of the first things that I learned about her was that, in addition to her extraordinary and absolutely original talent, Frida had a capacity for inspiring feelings of an exceptional intensity in almost anyone who encountered her. And she would seem to continue to do so, even in death. (I should here admit my own enthrallment, with which I seem to have infected my friends, Gloria and Mary.) Thus, a trip to the Frida Kahlo Museum, which was formerly her home, the blue house out in Coyoacán, is apt to have the character of a pilgrimage to a shrine. We went there to pay homage as well as out of curiosity. And we had, I am sure, like all passionate pilgrims, a burden of expectations, or preconceptions, some quite possibly unconscious.

In any case, the museum contained some vast surprises: considerable beauty, much sadness, and several disturbing questions.

The first surprise for me was quite simply the intensity of the color of those high outer walls; to a Californian (I suppose

I am one), the phrase "blue house" implies a pastel, surely not the violent, vibrant blue of Frida's house, which is like certain Mexican skies. Its size, too, was unexpected: It covers a small town block. High walls, then, and a gate guarded by two papier-mâché judas figures—and by a small, somewhat shabby real guard, who assures visitors that their entrance is free and warns them that they may not take pictures.

To the right, just as one passes between the judas giants, there is a small room with a glassed-in counter and some shelves, obviously designed as a bookstore-postcard display area—and now quite bare. Empty, that is, except for one rather gaudy pamphlet, entitled "Altar in the First Centenary of Diego Rivera," and in which there are many references to, and an introduction by, Dolores Olmeda, the "Life Director of the Diego Rivera and Frida Kahlo Museums." Frida is mentioned only once, as Diego's third wife. No books on Frida, no posters or postcards. (Why?)

The garden area that one next sees is rich and wonderful, however: a barely tamed green jungle, a perfect habitat for Frida's pet monkeys, for birds. (Cats would love it there, I thought, not seeing any.) At the time of my visit a large bed of pink lilies blossomed, the kind called Naked Ladies. And great tall trees. And a tangled profusion of vines.

On a wall near the entrance to Frida's house an inscription informed us that Frida and Diego had lived in this house from 1929 to 1954—a touching announcement and quite untrue (and who put it there, I wonder?). For although Frida was born in that house, which was built by her father, Diego's residences were both multiple and brief; he came and went very much as he chose, neither remaining at home nor staying away for long (one knows the type). The abode most lengthily shared by Frida and Diego is the two joined houses in San Angel, now the Diego Rivera Museum.

The first room of the blue house is rather low and small,

as are all the rooms in this semicolonial sprawl. One can imagine the house as warm and wonderful, hospitable first to the large Kahlo group (her father by two wives had six daughters), and then to Frida and Diego and their enormous circle of friends: Trotsky, Siqueiros, et cetera. But it takes considerable imagining, so little household furniture is left (and whatever happened to it? Where are all the ordinary tables and chairs that were used by Frida?).

Frida's paintings line this entrance room, and while interesting and highly original, as is all her work, they are simply not her best; in no sense is this a major Kahlo exhibition—a great pity, since her work is extremely hard to find. Most of her paintings are in private collections, including all the paintings that she willed to Rivera and that he in turn willed to a trust for the people of Mexico, along with her house. She is barely represented in museums in Mexico City.

The most striking of that small collection is the bright still life of watermelons, *Viva la Vida,* thus titled and signed by Frida very shortly before her death. But this painting's appeal seems emotional and historic, rather than intrinsic.

The kitchen is cozily furnished indeed, with bright painted chairs, red and yellow, new-looking (too new to have been there when Frida was), the sort that one might find in any Mexican open market. And glazed plates and pottery, cooking implements. Tiny jars affixed to the back wall, high up, spell out *Frida y Diego* in large letters. This seemed an unlikely note of kitsch, and indeed I was later told that these names were a later addition, put up some years after the deaths of Diego and Frida.

Other rooms house an extensive collection of pre-Columbian figures, and paintings, mostly by Rivera, some by friends, both Mexican and European. And there is Diego's bedroom, with his surprisingly small bed for such a huge man, and his rough, enormous boots. Then, going upstairs, within the broad, dark stairwell is the vast collection of *retalbos,* small Mexican votive paintings, said to have profoundly influenced the art of Frida.

And then one comes to Frida's tiny, narrow, poignant bedroom, the room in which, at forty-seven, she died and was laid out. And photographed, lying there.

Since she was so very, very often photographed in life (more often than Marilyn Monroe, it has been said)—the daughter of a photographer, she must have been early habituated to what seems to many people an intrusion—it is not surprising that she was also photographed in death, on this same narrow white bed, with its florally embroidered sheets. One of the terrible plaster casts that she finally had to wear (and that she decorated with painted flowers) lies on the coverlet. Still, this sense of her death makes visiting this area both macabre and embarrassing: I felt that I should not have been there.

It seems more permissible to enter the studio, built for her by Diego, in 1946, and wonderfully open to views of her wild green garden. It is a cheering, open room, and one can forgive Diego a great deal for having built this space for Frida's work.

Which leads us to a question that often seems to trouble Frida's partisans: Why did Frida remain in such a state of adoration for a man who was continuously, compulsively unfaithful to her, and who was for long periods of time conspicuously off and away with other, often famous, women? It seems to me that there are two explanations, insofar as one can "explain" a major passion—one rational, one not. The rational explanation would be that Diego entirely supported Frida's work; he often spoke of her as one of the greatest living painters, he cited the intensely female, anguished complexity of her work. He even compared his own painting unfavorably to hers (quite correctly, in my own view).

And, more darkly, irrationally, Frida was absolutely addicted to Diego; she could be said to have been impaled on her mania for Diego, as she had been literally impaled in the horrifying streetcar accident that, when she was 18, so painfully, horribly transformed her life. She herself referred to the "two accidents" in her life, the streetcar crash and Diego.

IN THE course of reading and thinking intensively about Frida Kahlo, one night I watched a TV special on Billie Holiday, and I sensed, I thought, a connection between the two women, whose life spans overlapped: They surely shared extremes of talent, as well as of personal beauty (Frida in photographs is much more beautiful than the self she painted) and addictiveness.

BUT FRIDA'S studio seems a lively, heartening place. Even the wheelchair placed before her easel seems emblematic of great courage, rather than of debility and pain.

THE DIEGO Rivera Museum, in San Angel—it is almost adjacent to the very posh, very beautiful San Angel Inn—is quite another matter. Crowded with collections— pre-Columbian figures, folk art, paintings (none, significantly, by Frida Kahlo)—and with furniture, it is meticulously kept up. Frida's house, adjoining, linked to Diego's by a high cross-walk that she sometimes closed off—Frida's house in San Angel is closed, roped off, forbidden. There is even a curious eroticism present in this homage to Diego, this shrine: In one room a chair that is obviously Diego's, with his boots on the floor, a coat flung over the back—this Diego chair faces a large portrait of a sexily semiundressed young woman, whose transported eyes stare raptly at the Maestro.

The basement bookstore is richly filled with postcards and posters and books, representing both Diego and Frida. There are even copies of the marvelously gotten-out new biography of Frida by the Mexican printer-publisher and Kahlo scholar, Martha Zamora, recently published in the States.

TWO WORDS often used in connection with Kahlo are *narcissism* ("All those self-portraits") and *masochism* ("All that blood"). Both seem to me quite wrongly applied. I rather believe that Kahlo painted herself and her images of personal pain in an effort to stave off madness and death, a desperate enterprise in which she was hardly alone and in which she was not entirely successful—as who can ever be, for good?

I HAVE recently read that there are no longer any Frida Kahlo paintings in her house—and I do not plan to go there again, it is simply too sad.

But this fall, the fall of 1990, it is rumored that Dolores Olmeda will open her house, La Feria, in the Xochimilco district of Mexico City (not far from Coyoacán) as a museum, featuring 137 works by Diego and 25 by Frida. As one report has described it: "Sequestered in a tiny courtyard room removed from the main galleries, they [the Kahlos] seem reduced to a mere supporting role. Passing between the two

areas is like going from Charles Dickens to Emily Dickinson."
(*Connoisseur,* October 1990)

I can only say that were I forced to make such an odd literary choice, I would inevitably choose Ms. Dickinson.

Dolores Olmeda's acquisition of the Kahlos and her subsequent removal of them from the blue house has a somewhat odd history: She got several Kahlos from the widow of the Mexican ambassador, Eduardo Morillo Safa, because the Bank of Mexico, which was supposed to get them, had defaulted on the sale. And Olmeda did this because, she said, Diego, in tears, had begged her to do so. The problem is that at the time of this sale Diego was already dead; also, Olmeda is known to have intimate and extensive connections with the Bank of Mexico. It is all very murky and very (unhappily) Mexican.

In the same article that so vividly describes the placement of the Kahlos in the new museum, Olmeda is quoted as saying, "I didn't like Frida. We were different. She was a lesbian, you know, and I didn't like that. I don't like her paintings. They are very trashy. I admire her very much, but I was never a friend of hers." (Perhaps it was just as well for Frida not to have had such a friend?)

But I plan to visit that museum and to see all those Kahlos—soon.